from the

Advertizer

1849-1870

The clock on the old Post Office (now Prezzo's) on Church Street, put there in memory of John Askew Roberts, the first editor of the Advertiser

The story of Oswestry told through the

Advertizer
1849-1870

compiled by Neil Rhodes

THIS CLOCK WAS ERECTED BY
PUBLIC SUBSCRIPTION ON JUNE 24th 1890,
IN MEMORY OF
JOHN ASKEW ROBERTS J.P.
FOUNDER OF THE ADVERTIZER.
BORN OSWESTRY 1826 DIED OSWESTRY 1884.

The inscription on the plaque under the clock on the old Post Office; this is not the original inscription.

Published by Neil Rhodes Books

Well Cottage
Wern
Llanymynech
SY22 6PF

nr@neilrhodes.co.uk

www.neilrhodesbooks.com

Edited by Jeremy Smith

British Library Cataloguing in Publication Data

A catalogue record for this book is available from the British Library

ISBN 978-0-9555557-2-5

Printed by Counter Print
Stafford
ST16 3AX
01785 241404
www.counterprint.co.uk

CONTENTS

The site of the Albion Printing Office on Bailey Head, where the Advertiser was published until 1858

by
NONNA WOODWARD

This book has been written to mark and celebrate the 160 years of history bound up in the Advertizer newspaper. It is unusual for a local paper still to be thriving after so many years but the Thomas family, owners of the newspaper, have been strong in their support of the paper and the town through most of those years. Indeed many will remember Rowland and his son Eric as characters of the town, and they held strong the view that the independence of the local paper keeps the spirit of the town healthy and vital. The family have supported that view by fighting to keep the company NWN Media flourishing too, and have invested recently in a new state-of-the-art press on which the Advertizer is printed, thus preserving that independence.

The desire to glean information goes back a long way, and in this book the author weaves together the web of history of the railways, the Advertizer and the characters of Oswestry town, giving the reader a delightful insight into the ups and downs of life as it was in those days. The fascinating detail of the articles lets us live alongside the inhabitants, showing the politics and the problems of the day.

And has life changed very much from those days? The trials and tribulations of the development and growth of the newspaper reflected the events that were happening then. Today we have similar hurdles to jump and hoops to negotiate. Reading how our forefathers created the newspaper reminds us that life has never been easy - but how grateful we should be that they persevered. They fought bureaucracy and politics, they fought for advertising and the right to print opinion and news freely and in the end – however much they wished to give the service freely - they recognised the need to charge for the paper too. They had set the foundations and framework for today.

NONNA WOODWARD, vice chairman of NWN Media Ltd

The Albion Printing Office on Bailey Head in the 1850s

INTRODUCTION

Looking through old copies of the OSWESTRY ADVERTISER, it is surprising to find so many similarities between now and a century and a half ago. The local concerns are often the same – crime, drinking, the state of the streets – even if some of our attitudes have changed, especially towards the rich and famous. This book contains a selection of some of the more interesting or unusual items about Oswestry, and on the way reveals something of the history of the town.

The OSWESTRY ADVERTISER has a long and auspicious history. It started as little more than a monthly publication of railway times for the town of Oswestry. It grew into a large newspaper featuring news from all over Shropshire and North Wales, as well as national items.

The first issue of the OSWESTRY ADVERTISER AND RAILWAY GUIDE (note the s in Advertiser, unlike the present Advertizer with a z – the name changed in the course of the period of this book) was published on Friday, January 5, 1849. The first issues were published monthly, and consisted of just ten pages, each page being a mere seven inches by four inches — smaller than this page.

It was printed at premises on the corner of Albion Hill and Bailey Street (now the Flower Gallery). The owner of the company was Samuel Roberts, though his sons William Whitridge and John Askew were the primary movers in the idea of a newspaper. Askew Roberts eventually became the chief editor.

The Advertiser was not the first newspaper in Oswestry, there being a short-lived one called the OSWESTRY HERALD, published in 1820 by William Cathrall (writer of the *History of Oswestry*). The Herald was a Tory paper, while the Advertiser was definitely liberal and non-conformist, like its owners. The only newspaper in Shropshire before the Advertiser was the SHREWSBURY CHRONICLE, founded in 1772, but there had been other publications, including Samuel Roberts' OSWALD'S WELL, a very small magazine that featured much that was later in the Advertiser. Apart from the railway timetable, the Advertiser also printed many advertisements, an 'Almanack' for each month, and some letters, but hardly any news, as the Stamp Act taxed any papers with news, to enable the government to suppress free comment.

The railways had a huge importance at the time, and it was no coincidence that the first edition of the OSWESTRY ADVERTISER was published only a few days after the first railway in Oswestry was opened. Railways were opening up the country, allowing speeds of 30mph when stagecoaches averaged only about 7mph. Now that the line from Oswestry to Gobowen had been built, connecting Oswestry with the Chester to Shrewsbury line, it was now possible to travel by train to Manchester, Liverpool and London. The journey to London now took only eight hours, unlike the two or more days by road.

But the Oswestry to Gobowen line was a branch line, the Great Western Railway main line having bypassed Oswestry, as various local landowners hadn't wanted a railway to go through their fields. Huge efforts were then made to put Oswestry on a main line, the favourite idea being a line from Manchester to the port of Milford Haven. This would have greatly benefitted Oswestry, and the Advertiser continually supported the building of such a line.

This was just one of the campaigns the newspaper conducted. It deplored the severity of the anti-poaching laws, especially as the magistrates were landowners. It printed many articles against drunkenness in the town, to little effect, apparently. It attempted to see that roads were made with proper surfaces, especially in the poorer parts of the town.

From its small beginnings it grew to be a paper read over a large area, in just 21 years.

ACKNOWLEDGEMENTS

Many people have helped in writing this book and collecting the pictures. I would like to thank, in particular:
Nonna Woodward for writing the foreword
Su Perry
Jeremy Smith
Derek Williams and the staff of Oswestry Library
Sue Jones, Brenda Jones and Mal Humphreys for help and copies of old newspapers

BOOKS CONSULTED INCLUDE:

Oswestry, by Isaac Watkin
Street Names of Oswestry, by John Pryce-Jones (and others of his very useful books)
The Advertizer Family, by Robbie Thomas
The Story of the Cambrian, by C. P. Gasquoine
The Cambrian Railways, by Rex Christiansen & R W Miller
The Cambrian Railways, by R W Kidner
History of Oswestry, by William Cathrall

Throughout this book I have mainly restricted reports to the town of Oswestry itself, with only a few exceptions for important events. Everything in this font – Oswestry Advertiser – is taken from the Advertiser. Almost always the reports are excerpts, but to make it easier to read I have not indicated where cuts have been made. I have tried as much as possible to reproduce exactly the printing style of the Advertiser, with their *italics* and SMALL CAPITALS where they have used them. I have generally kept the original spelling, only correcting what are obviously printer's errors. Anything within [*square brackets*] is my addition. The advertisements are all from the Advertiser of the time.

NEIL RHODES

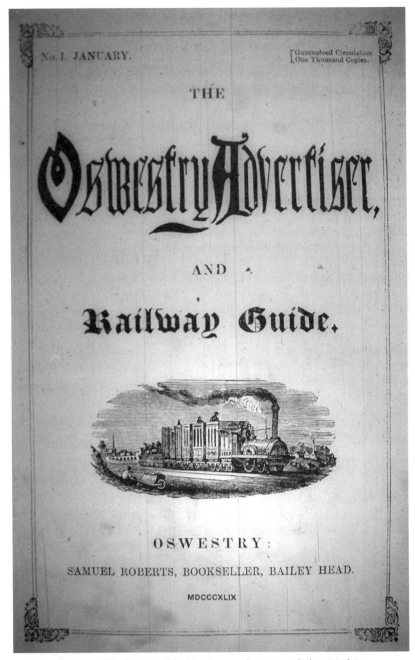

No. I. JANUARY.

Guaranteed Circulation
One Thousand Copies.

THE

Oswestry Advertiser,

AND

Railway Guide.

OSWESTRY:

SAMUEL ROBERTS, BOOKSELLER, BAILEY HEAD.

MDCCCXLIX

The cover of the first copy of the Advertiser — and at very nearly the original size.

These were the very first words of the Advertiser, an editorial, though under the heading:

NOTICES TO CORRESPONDENTS, &c.

Our present publication is necessarily imperfect, and may possibly in some departments be erroneous. None who have ever endeavoured to collect information from original sources, will be surprised at this, for they will know and appreciate the difficulties in the way of such a search. We hope, by degrees, to fill out the defective, and correct the inaccurate departments; so as to approximate as nearly as may be to the ideal we have set before us—"a complete compendium of useful local information."

This was the typical style of the Advertiser at the time, with very long sentences. There then followed a cryptic little piece that suggested much but told little:

PHILOMEL.—The late John Jones, Esq. of the Rhos, is no more. He departed this life on the 15th of last month, and not even the plaints of *Philomel* can now reach his ear. He expired suddenly, in the vigour of his days; and an inquest should have been held over him. The matter was, however, hushed up; in order to spare his sorrowing friend the disagreeable publicity of an investigation, and in tenderness to the reputation of the guilty parties who brought the deceased to an unnatural and untimely end.

No more was ever said about the mysterious death of John Jones, or why the matter was hushed up. The third comment was rather a strange request, considering this was the first edition:

AN OSWESTRIAN.—We would willingly meet our correspondent's wishes by enlarging publication, and devoting more space to literature and some to politics, did circumstances justify the step. To be enabled to do so *we must have more advertisements*. It is quite impossible to give a quantity of paper and printing away, unless the return from the advertising department compensates for the loss.

January, 1849

There followed a full page almanac, two pages of railways timetables, two of advertisements, and a few pages of letters, poetry, jokes, and odd facts. That layout continued throughout 1849. This is a part of a very long (three pages) letter from September:

The first editor of the Advertiser,
John Askew Roberts

The Almanack of the Month.

DECEMBER.—XXXI DAYS.

THIS month is so called from having been originally the tenth month of the Roman year. By our Saxon forefathers it was styled, *Winter Monath*, and *Giul eora*, ere or first yule; but after their conversion to Christianity the name was changed to *Heligh Monath*, or Holy Month. On the 15th, *Chisleu*, (the third month of the civic, and the ninth of the sacred Hebrew year,) which commenced November 16th, ends, and is succeeded by *Tebeth*, which continues till January 23rd. In the Greek calendar we find *Poseideon*, the sixth month, so called in honour of *Poseidon*, or Neptune, to whom a solemn sacrifice, called *Oneilion*, was offered at this season. The Mohammedan year 1266 A.H. commenced November 17th. The first month is *Moharrem*. On December 17th, *Safar* begins.

MD	WD	HISTORICAL AND BIOGRAPHICAL MEMORANDA.
1	S	Anna Comnena b. 1083. Leo X. d. 1521.
2	S	1st Sun. in Advent. Battle of Austerlitz. 1805.
3	M	James II. abd. 1688. R. Bloomfield b. 1766
4	T	Dr. Burney b. 1757. Card. Richelieu d. 1642
5	W	Mozart d. 1792. Marshel Ney shot. 1815.
6	Th	Monk b. 1608. H. Jenkins d. æt. 169. 1670.
7	F	Algernon Sydney beh. 1683. Flaxman d. 1826
8	S	R. Baxter d. 1691. Elihu Burritt b. 1811.
9	S	2nd Sun. in Advent. John Milton b. 1608.
10	M	W. Lloyd Garrison b. 1805
11	T	Charles XII. killed. 1718. Gay d. 1732.
12	W	Lord Hood b. 1724. Dr. Darwin b 1732.
13	Th	Hen. IV. France b. 1553. Dr. Johnson d. 1781
14	F	General Washington d. 1799.
15	S	Lavater b. 1741. Izaak Walton d. 1683.
16	S	3rd Sun. in Advent. Cromwell dec. Protector,
17	M	Earl Stanhope d. 1816. [1653. Selden b. 1584
18	T	Sir Humphrey Davy b. 1778. [yer b 1699.
19	W	Ember Week. Tycho Brahe b. 1546. W. Bow-
20	Th	Gray b. 1716. Louis Napoleon procl. Pres.
21	F	St. Thomas. [of the French Rep 1848.
22	S	T. Banks b. 1738 Wollaston d. 1828.
23	S	4th Sun. in Advent. Arkwright b. 1732.
24	M	Bp. Warburton b. 1698. Crabbe b. 1754.
25	T	Christmas Day. Wm Collins b. 1720.
26	W	St. Stephen. Sir Isaac Newton b. 1642.
27	Th	St. John. Kepler b. 1571. C. Lamb d. 1834.
28	F	Innocents. Dr. Burney d. 1817. Bayle d. 1706
29	S	Thos. à Becket ass. 1171. Wycliffe d. 1384
30	S	1st Sun. aft. Xtmas. Soc. Jesuits found. 1535
31	M	Royal Society inst. 1660. Boerhaave b. 1668

SEASONABLE NOTES.

ASTRONOMICAL.—On the 21st the Sun enters Capricornus, and winter commences. *Mercury* is a morning star in the earlier part of the month. *Venus* and *Jupiter* are morning stars through the whole month. *Mars* is visible throughout the night; he is in the constellation Gemini till the 10th, and in Taurus to the end of the month, when he sets as the sun rises. *Saturn* is an evening star, and is near the moon on the 22nd.

THE MOON'S CHANGES.

Last Quarter 6th day, 6h. 53m. aft.
New - - 14th day, 3h. 38m. aft.
1st Quarter 23rd day, 7h. 40m. aft.
Full - - 29th day, 2h. 0m. aft.

THE WEATHER.—The characteristics of this month are in the main similar to those of the last; i. e. generally warm, stormy, and wet. If winter sets in at all this month, it does not usually come in all its rigour until on or after the 25th. Should the wind be E. or N.E. settled frost may be looked for; but the S. W. winds are now sometimes violent, attended with heavy rain, and occasionally with thunder. If snow falls in the last week of December, it is frequently of great depth. The mean temperature of the month is usually about 40 degs. The mole throws up hillocks, rats and mice become troublesome in houses, the fox seeks the farmyard in quest of poultry, sky-larks and fieldfares are seen in flocks, especially in snowy weather, and snipes may be shot in great numbers. In mild weather a few moths appear and gnats dance in the open air. The mean temperature of the whole year is not found to vary, in different years, more than 4 degrees and a half.

FLORICULTURAL.—The business of this month will consist in finishing all intended winter planting, and forwarding the requisite pruning of trees and shrubs. Pruning must be particularly attended to in all roses, except the China. It is a mistake to think that by closely pruning the number of flowers will be lessened. Standard roses require to be very closely pruned, in order to make them form a uniform and compact head, cutting the young shoots annually to within two or three inches of the part they started from. All the varieties of this beautiful flowering shrub require an abundance of the best rotted cow and horse manure to be applied regularly. Protect delicate roots from severe frost by strewing ashes, sand, or litter over them, and auriculas from heavy rains. Clear the plants in pots within doors from all decayed leaves and shoots; they will occasionally require a little water, but it must be given very sparingly.

CIVIL AND POLITICAL.—31st. "*Last day of the year*. Those who have not been accustomed to keep an account of their personal or household expences should begin from this day. Those in trade who have not been accustomed to take an annual account of stock should begin from this day. Without cash-books and stock-books trade is little better than a game of chance."—*British Almanac.*

The Almanack, printed each month, gave dates of famous historical events, the derivation of the name of the month, some astronomical information, notes on the weather, and gardening tips.

LETTERS ON LOCAL MATTERS. NO. 1.—IMPROVEMENTS.

DEAR SIR.—My own memory does not extend over half a century. It may reasonably be conjectured, that were an Oswestrian, who took leave of his beloved town before the commencement of that century which has now run well-nigh half its course, to revisit it at the present day, he would be completely and bewilderingly astonished by the altered aspect of the place he knew so well. Its ancient Church tower, indeed, and its more ancient Castle hill, he would find much as when his fleshly eyes loved to linger upon them. In general outline plan, also, he might perhaps detect some resemblance to the Oswestry of his mortal life, but in all besides, how changed! what havoc of the old familiar scenes! what altered forms! what new sights and modern innovations! How odd, too, the investments [*clothes*] of the people that throng the thoroughfares. How strangely men shuffle along in those long loose lower garments, hiding alike symmetry and deformity! And how much smarter the ladies are!

We may wonder what caused such huge changes in Oswestry between 1800 and 1849 that made everyone look so different. The correspondent explained: the reason was the arrival of the railway in the town:

Many towns have suffered from the proximity of a railroad; Oswestry hitherto has reaped nothing but benefit. The facilities for free and cheap locomotion afforded to individuals are no small advantage to our active townsmen. The tradesman who formerly contented himself with an excursion to Shrewsbury or Liverpool once a year, now regularly visits the London and Manchester markets; and if particularly enterprising deems it no formidable matter to go now and then in pursuit of bargains to continental or even transatlantic shores. The lady who in bygone days found it difficult to coax her loving lord into an autumnal trip to Admaston or Llangollen, now thinks nothing of Brighton or the Highlands; and in a little while even Baden-Baden and the Alps will fail to satisfy their craving for fresh air. A watering place on the Red Sea, or a pic-nic in the Himalayas, will then become indispensable.

I am, Yours very sincerely, Timetes
September, 1849

The Advertiser at this time was free, so it was necessary to assure advertisers of its circulation:

In consequence of misconception respecting the extent of the circulation of the Oswestry Advertiser, the Publisher deems it right to state, that not more than half of the impression (1000 copies) is distributed in the town. The remaining 500 are circulated chiefly among the gentry and farmers residing within 10 miles of Oswestry; and a number of copies is forwarded regularly to the Solicitors, Auctioneers, and other gentlemen in the neighbouring towns.

December, 1849

In January 1850 the Advertiser became larger, a quarto sheet of eight pages, each nine inches by seven, with three columns as opposed to two:

> Our readers will see that we have this month altered our form, though not our essential character or objects. Our new shape will, however, enable us to pay more attention that we have hitherto done to general literature and local correspondence.
> *January, 1850*

Poetry featured in almost every edition of the Advertiser. Here is a typical example:

TO MISS ——

Pride is on thy brow, lady,
Scorn is in thine eye,
Looks of coldness thou dost cast
On those who pass thee by;
High by birth and rank, lady,
Lovely though thou be
Yet for this I would not wish
To change my lot with thee.

Sweet's the bread which labour
Earns, with honest hands,
And sweet the cup affection fills,
Quaffed in contentment's bands;
But sweeter far than all, lady,

The pleasure to be found
In knowing that we have not been
The cumberers of the ground.

The happy not always found,
Midst rank and wealth and power,
But oft the cankerworm is found,
Lodged in the sweetest flower;
Then smooth thy brow so proud, lady,
And not so scornful be:
With all thy rank and beauty, lady,
I do not envy thee.
July, 1850

One of the campaigns of the Advertiser was for the early closing for shops; the hours seem to have been even longer than they are now, and shops had to remain open at the whim of any customer who wanted something:

> We are happy to hear that the Tradesmen of Oswestry have agreed to close their shops at 7 o'clock during the winter months. The evils of the Late-Hour System have been long and ably denounced, and, who should have thought, ere this the public mind would have been so far alive to the subject as to prevent the necessity of the tradesmen issuing a placard to announce the determination

TO THE LADIES OF OSWESTRY.

MORRIS & SAVIN beg respectfully to inform the Ladies of Oswestry and its vicinity, that they have just received a fresh supply of Messrs. JAMES McLINTOCK and Co.'s Improved FRENCH WOVE CORSETS; they possess a decided superiority over any yet offered to the public on account of their varied excellencies, and are highly worthy of examination and trial.

M. & S. call particular attention to their Stock of Victoria Wool Knitted Paletots, in all sizes and colours.

They have also a large assortment of Lace and Embroidered Muslin Dresses, for evening wear.

French Flowers and Head Dresses.

An advertisement for the draper's shop, Morris & Savin, the M&S of its day. This is one of the first references to the soon-to-be famous local man, Thomas Savin, in his first career, as haberdasher.

to close at a reasonable hour. But this is not the case, still some thought-less people will "go a-shopping" at all sorts of unreasonable hours.
October, 1850

This letter took a long way round to express a complaint about the Great Western Railway station of 1850, suggesting it ought to be sent from the town to The Great Exhibition in London:

MR EDITOR.—I am not given to dreaming, yet nevertheless one night last week, just after I had completed my third tumbler of brandy and water, and was cosily sitting on my easy chair by the side of a cheerful fire, and opposite to my no less cheerful "better half", I experienced something very nearly approaching to a dream. I had been reading of the Great Exhibition, when a ghostly visitant appeared before me.

After some conversation, he said that was I really desirous of making Oswestry notorious, then urge upon his worshipful the Mayor and the Town Council, the advisability of sending up for the inspection of an admiring world our Railway Station—which he would pledge itself was such a building as never in the whole course of his professional career had he encountered!

Mr Smuggins wondered rather ironically if after seeing the presumably dreadful station the Crystal Palace itself (the huge building made of glass where the Great Exhibition was held, in Hyde Park) would seem inadequate. But more importantly:

What should we do without our Station while it was in London? he replied that we might do equally well with a few *hogsheads* [large barrels], which he had no doubt would be kindly lent by the Grocers on such an occasion; but he would strongly recommend us *to have a new one built* for that probably were ours to go to London, we might have some difficulty in obtaining it back again. With this my visitor disappeared, and I was made alive to the existing realities by my wife pulling my nose and telling me that I was making myself very disagreeable by snoring so loud.

Your obedient servant,
TONY SMUGGINS
December, 1850

The changing cover of the Advertiser; this one is for November 1850, with the motto: TRUTH AND TRADE—LIFE'S HIGHER AND LOWER INTERESTS

Up until now the Advertiser had been free, but that changed in 1851:

OUR STATE AND PROSPECTS.

It is with no small feelings of gratification we commence the third year of publication. Many were the predictions, when we started, as to the probable duration of our existence, the most sanguine of which did not allow us more than twelve months. The two years existence of the Oswestry Advertiser has not, however, been productive of £. s. d. to the Proprietor. And when we state that during this period, the *Stamp Duties* and *Postages* have amounted to nearly SIXTY POUNDS, and that *Twenty Five Thousand copies* have been given away, this will not be wondered at. Such being the case, in future, in order to receive the ADVERTISER, regularly, for twelve months, One Shilling, in advance, must be paid.

We purpose, in future, to eschew *Politics*. There is no lack of subject of *local interest*, that will always be sufficient to fill columns, without meddling with "vexed questions," which never have, and never will be settled.

January, 1851

It's difficult to say if the next correspondent's name is a coincidence or a pseudonym, but the state of the Castle Bank would become something of an obsession with the town for a long time:

Thomas Hillock writes to complain of the Castle Hill being enclosed, and the gate leading to it locked. We would recommend to him, and all who think with him, that the closing of the Castle Hill from the public is an infringement to our rights. Remove the gate from its hinges whenever you want to breathe the pure air, and enjoy the splendid viewpoint from Castle Hill, and you may rest assured that the parties who have caused the Hill to be enclosed will, if they have "law" on their side, very soon let you know by what authority they lock the Gate.

April, 1851

The state of the streets was a constant topic. In 1851 the people in charge of the roads were the Street Commissioners:

LOCAL IMPROVEMENTS.

Strangers entering Oswestry are continually enquiring, why the causeways [*pavements*] are not flagged? The cry is echoed by our townsfolk in stronger language, and we often hear them indignantly explain that "it's a shame we should be compelled to walk on a rough pavement when we can get stone so cheap." They seem to think, that could we get our worthy Commissioners to "move" on the subject, it would greatly facilitate their own movements from one end of Oswestry to the other.

August, 1851

The newly enlarged Advertiser's Christmas supplement for 1850

Pitcher Bank is the area between the Castle Bank and the present library and Council offices; clearly it was in a very different state from now, as Philip Henry Dicker, a local doctor who lived nearby, wrote:

A HINT TO OUR TOWN COUNCIL.

SIR.—If anyone doubt the speciality of the Providence which protects young children from sudden death, let him observe them, as I do daily, charging in "shoals and motions" upon the very edge of that imminent deadly parapet wall bounding the Pitcher Bank. Sometimes, indeed, they "topple down headlong," but I have not heard of any serious accident. Children of older growth, however, frequently fall over this most dangerous and unfenced descent, and you were present, a few days since, when a son of one of our most respected tradesmen, seized with an epileptic fit fell over into the street, and received severe injuries. I hope the authorities will see into this, and that it will not require one chairman and six common council men to fall down this precipice before they feel the necessity to make a motion for an amendment.

I am, Sir, yours truly, PHILIP HENRY DICKER, Chapel House
September, 1851

Charging money for the Advertiser seemed to have been successful:

ENLARGEMENT OF THE OSWESTRY ADVERTISER.

We are happy to state, that although some parties were offended, our circulation considerably increased. When we gave the Advertiser away our circulation was principally confined to the town of Oswestry and its immediate neighbourhood, now however we are continually receiving orders from neighbouring towns and villages, to which when we circulated gratuitously we could not respond, as our number (one thousand) was not sufficient to spread far enough for this purpose.

November, 1851

With only one railway branch line to Oswestry, coaches were still important, so their times were also printed. Looking at the times (four hours from Oswestry to Newtown) and fares (11 shillings then was worth the equivalent of about £20 now) it's easy to see here why more railways were so desired:

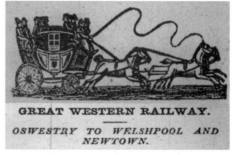

GREAT WESTERN RAILWAY.

OSWESTRY TO WELSHPOOL AND NEWTOWN.

OSWESTRY, WELSHPOOL, AND NEWTOWN. The Royal Oak leaves Oswestry daily at 3.30 o'clock p.m. and arrives at Newtown about 7.30 o'clock. Leaves the Bear's Head Hotel, Newtown, at 8.15 a.m. arriving in Oswestry at 11.30. *Fares*—To Newtown, Inside 11 shillings. Outside 7 shillings. To Welshpool, Inside 6 shillings. Outside 3 shillings and 6 pence.

1852 started with a project to convert the Castle Bank into an arboretum, paid for by local subscriptions:

> We are happy to be able to report progress satisfactorily on the proposed improvements at the Castle Bank. The same zeal which originated the movement keeps it in activity, and bids fair to bring it to a speedy and auspicious completion. We understand that a model of the Castle Bank, *as it is to be*, has been constructed, and a contract entered into for the execution of the plan, and a meeting was held in the Council Chamber, on Thursday last, for the purpose of obtaining assent and support to the measures proposed.
> *February, 1852*

Oswald's Well must have been a popular visitor's attraction, though it may not have been in the best state. This letter complains that it ought to receive the same treatment as the Castle Bank:

> WHAT AILS OSWALD'S WELL?
>
> Strange murmurs have lately been heard to proceed from Oswald's Well. Voices of complaint and expostulation have been heard in the vicinity, and we gather that the sainted well seems struggling to gurgle out some plea for its own restoration and protection.
>
> "The Castle Bank is a relic of antiquity, is it?" quoth the hoary complainant; "I beg it may be understood that I can remember the Castle Bank when it was no Castle Bank at all, but only a green hill for barbarous Britons to keep their sheep upon. Before a stone of those crumbling ruins was laid, I was gushing up here, living and fresh, the same pure, cool spring you see me today, and I think it rather hard that so-called antiquities, which beside me are quite useful, only a poor thousand years old or so, should be put over my head in this manner.
>
> "You are proud of my age, you boast of my salubrity, you bring strangers to see me as one of your cheap curiosities, and yet you leave me neglected and ruinous, trampled and soiled by the very cattle of the field, and my

VOL. I. No. 4.]　　JANUARY, 1848.　　[PRICE 2D.

A cover of Samuel Roberts' precursor to the Advertiser, showing an engraving of Oswald's Well

19

fair channels choked and defiled by weeds and noisome impurities."
April, 1852

Sir Watkin Williams Wynn was the 6th Baronet. He was Member of Parliament for Denbighshire from 1841 until his death in 1885, aged 64. The seat had previously been held by his father, grandfather and great-grandfather, all of whom were also named Watkin Williams Wynn. His wife was a cousin, and also a Williams Wynn:

Sir Watkin Wiliams Wynn in later years

NUPTIALS OF SIR W. W. WYNN, BARONET. Disbursements of the subscription collected for Festivities and Rejoicings and Charitable Distribution in the town and neighbourhood of Oswestry on the happy event of the Marriage of Sir Watkin and Lady Williams Wynn.
May, 1852

Oswestry had been bypassed by the Great Western Railway. Local people were now insistent that Oswestry should be on a main line, a line that should go to the then very important port of Milford Haven:

Our readers are probably aware that there are two projects before the public on establishing railway communication between Manchester and the North of England and South Wales. One of these projects contemplates the construction of a line from Shrewsbury to Aberystwyth with a branch line to Oswestry, from a place beyond Welshpool; the other project is to carry the main trunk line through Oswestry to Newtown. It is clear that communication must ultimately extend to Milford Haven. No person who will take the trouble of inspecting a map of England and Wales can for a moment question, that the most advantageous communication for all parties must provide that the main trunk line shall pass through Oswestry.
August, 1852

Some progress was being made on improving the streets:

FLAGGING OF THE CAUSEWAYS.—At a meeting of the Commissioners of Oswestry held the other day, it was resolved to flag the side pavements of Brook-street, from Longueville and Williams's; Church-street, from the Sun Corner; and Beatrice-street, from Mr Parry's.
August, 1852

In June 1853 the Advertiser was again enlarged, from three to five columns a page, so it was now 13 by 20 inches, about the size of a present broadsheet paper like the Telegraph or Guardian. It was only one sheet, folded to make four pages, but many more reports were included. The New Year editorial had a very portentous feel:

THE YEAR MDCCCLIII.

The year 1853 opens, like its predecessors, on a world where good and evil, truth and falsehood, suffering and enjoyment, cross and intertwine in strange and almost fearful contrast. Yet hope is stronger than fear, and the light which rests upon the future, claims to be mightier and more enduring than the darkness.

January, 1853

Throughout the early years of the Advertiser there were many similar accidents to this one – as frequent as car accidents today. This report of an inquest held at The Boar's Head Inn into the death of a druggist, Mr Richard Evans, told of how he fell from his horse and died after the animal was spooked by dogs:

Patrick Collins, of Willow-street, hawker, was the first witness called. He stated that on the afternoon of Sunday he was returning from Market Drayton with his dog cart drawn by three dogs; when he came near the bridge that carries the Oswestry and Gobowen railway over the Ellesmere Road, he saw the deceased coming to meet them on horseback; witness and his wife were riding on the dog cart, and going at the rate of about three miles an hour; but the horse Mr Evans was riding became restive as it came near the dogs; witness got off the cart, drew the dogs to the side of the road, and went to the assistance of the deceased; witness asked if he should lead the horse past the dogs, to which Mr Evans replied, "I shall be glad if you will, the pony is rather unruly to-day"; Collins laid hold of the bridle, when the horse immediately reared up, broke from witness's hold, and threw Mr Evans upon his head on the road; the horse then galloped off; Collins lifted the unfortunate deceased upon his knee, and found him bleeding from the head and nose; there was a small pool of blood upon the spot where he fell.

In the report the Coroner then described the practice of using dogs and drawing carts as 'a very dangerous nuisance'. The man with the dog cart comes in for some strong criticism, despite his attempt to be helpful:

Owing to the barking of dogs and the great rate at which they were driven, there was scarcely any horse that would quietly meet them. Here was the case in which three poor dogs had been compelled to draw a cart, carry a man and his wife sixty-two miles in twenty-six hours, and owing to the desecration of the sabbath, a respectable tradesman of Oswestry, who was going to a place of worship at Whittington, had lost his life, and left three little children fatherless and motherless.

The jury returned a verdict of accidental death.

June, 1853

This is one of the earliest meetings for building a railway from Oswestry to Newtown, then called the Montgomeryshire Railway:

At a numerously attended Public Meeting held at the Guildhall, Oswestry, on Thursday the 23rd of June, 1853, "For the purpose of considering the propriety of petitioning the House of Lords in support of the Montgomeryshire Railway," the subjoined resolutions were unanimously adopted.

First,—"that in the opinion of this meeting a railway from the town of Oswestry to Welshpool to the town of Newtown, in the County of Montgomery, will be of essential service to the interests of this town and neighbourhood; and that the bill for making the Montgomeryshire Railway, which has now passed the House of Commons, is the only line before Parliament capable of effecting this most desirable object."

The Advertiser stated that if a new line were built:

We could look forward to seeing a railway station at Oswestry which will no longer be the ugliest in England, or, considering the amount of traffic, the least convenient in the world.

July, 1853

Another constant theme was water, as there was no waterworks or sewage system in the town. The Dispensary, a kind of medical centre and pharmacy, was opened in 1829 in Lower Brook Street, but a new one was being built near that place:

We are happy to find that the merits of Water, pleaded more than once in the Advertiser, are likely to be soon recognized among us in a public and enduring than by the opening of the Baths connected with the Dispensary. We should expect to see the citizens of Oswestry flocking to Brook-street, some with pick and trowel to assist in the building, some with burdens of wood and stone as their offering towards so general and manifest a benefit.

July, 1853

IN SABLE, SQUIRREL, ERMINE, AND WHITE.

IN THREE SIZES.

MORRIS & SAVIN beg to call attention to their Stock of New Goods for the approaching season; which will be found well worthy the inspection of visitors. The favour of a call will oblige.

The Crimean War began on 28 March, when Britain and France declared war on Russia. Despite the Advertiser's declaration only to report local matters and 'eschew politics', a great deal of the paper was taken up with the war, for the next three years. But in Oswestry there were more important matters:

> DEAR SIR,—It is rumoured in the town that the new clock which is to be placed over the Market Hall, in the Cross, is to be called the "Borough Clock," and will be *warranted* as a faithful time-keeper! We have three public clocks already, which are often as widely apart in time as they are in localities, and a new clock that will really put us "up to the time o'day" will be hailed as a boon. Let me suggest that a lamp, with a strong reflector, be placed over this clock, that we may know by night, as well as by day, how to regulate our engagements. The lamp ought to be paid for by the borough, whose name the clock will bear.
> *January, 1854*

The clock above the Cross Market Hall (now the Edinburgh Woollen Mill);
the Latin means, according to Isaac Watkin:
'Time and money, space and weight,
By one fixed standard calculate.'

The baths and new Dispensary opened on May 1, and would clearly make a difference to at least one section of the town:

> It is possible to have too much of even so excellent a commodity as water, and we are almost afraid some of the readers of the *Advertiser* may be prepared to remind us of this fact when they see the subject of baths and bathing again brought forward in these pages. Nevertheless we shall venture to state, as a piece of information really important, and interesting to all well-wishers to the town, that the long projected Public baths are now nearly completed, and, with the exception of the swimming-bath, which will not be ready quite so soon, will be thrown open in the course of the present month. We rejoice to believe that the sect of the Unwashed is becoming daily smaller and more unpopular.
> *April, 1854*

As the Advertiser expanded, more court cases were reported, though the law was not precise on what constituted news in an unstamped paper. Askew Roberts decided to report county courts but not police courts. This case suggests the way magistrates thought when they decided on a sentence:

Anne Thomas pleaded *Guilty* of stealing a calf's liver, the property of *John Edwards*. In consequence of the prisoner having left her husband entirely by her own fault, and, as such, the theft not being the result of want, the sentence was *two months imprisonment with hard labour*.
April, 1854

The lock-up, or gaol, was on the site of Christ Church, opposite the present library. The footpath referred to here must be along the present Chapel Street:

FOOTPATH INTO THE HORSE MARKET.—Mr E. W. Thomas proposed that a footpath and style [*stile*] be made into the Horse Market, opposite the gaol, and stated that there had been a footpath there from time immemorial, until that gate was created there, and that no one ought to deprive the public of their rights to the footpath. The Town Clerk said that he would oppose the motion on the part of the owners of the property, and that they ought not to make a highway of their Horse Market.
June, 1854

One of the most frequent offences to come before the magistrates of the town was 'driving without reins', which meant that the horse presumably found its own way, perhaps a bit like driving a car while using a mobile phone:

Several waggoners were summoned for driving without reins, and it would be well, we think, were every master to enforce upon his servant the danger that is incurred by so doing, not only to the public but to his own pocket. In each case a fine, considerable to a labouring man, was inflicted. Such cases as they ought to be reported, as public warnings, and we wonder that although so many have, from time to time, been fined, that not a meeting passes without so large a proportion of the cases being for "driving without reins."
July, 1854

Another major concern in the town was prostitution. 'Under the walls' seems to be a euphemism for a brothel, or at least describes the place they were, on Salop Road, just outside English Walls:

TRAFFICKING IN WOMAN.
SIR,—The public journals of this week have held up to execration those wretches in the great metropolis, who make merchandise of woman. But those whose systematic wickedness has been exposed are *strangers in blood* to the unhappy victims that they import and trade in. In our own town there are, "under the walls," five houses in one row, three of these houses are known to the police as notorious brothels, not only where wretched females are "*harboured*," but where they are "*encouraged*" by their parents in their deadly occupation. Mothers may be seen continually, but more especially on market and fair days, prowling about their dens of infamy, looking out for prey for their poor, ruined, abandoned daughters—mere children in years, but beldames in vice.

Are we to shut our eyes and hold our peace at what is known to everyone? What are our mud-pools, pig-styes, slaughter-houses, however offensive they may be, compared to such a moral nuisance as the dens "under the walls".

I am, Sir, Your obedient servant, A Burgess

July, 1854

This is a typical example of the 1854 way of dealing with children, in the good old days:

Stealing Plums.—John Williams, a lad thirteen years of age, residing with his mother at Pentreclawdd, pleaded guilty to stealing some plums, the property of Mr John Jones, of Cross Lanes. The boy was reported by the policeman to be an unruly fellow, although so young, and the magistrate sentenced him to be flogged in the gaol.

October, 1854

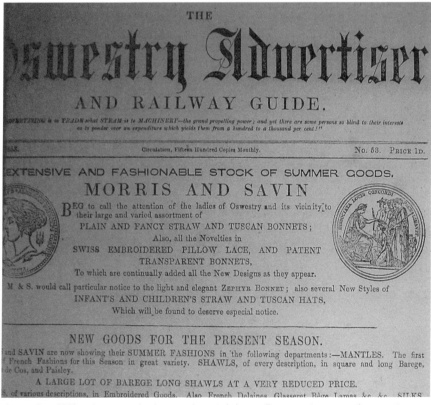

A cover from 1853, with a new and rather more long-winded motto: "ADVERTISING is to TRADE what STEAM is to MA-CHINERY—the grand propelling power; and yet there are some persons so blind to their interests as to ponder over an expenditure which yields them from a hundred to a thousand per cent!"

This editorial combines two of the commonest court cases, accidents on the road and drunkenness. Perhaps the Advertiser went too far in describing it as a 'scene of a very disgraceful exhibition of brutality and vice':

A poor lad fell under the wheels of his cart on the way to Maesbury, and received injuries of which he died in the course of a very few hours. It is said that the unfortunate sufferer had been drinking to excess, and that the fall was a consequence of his intoxication. He had boasted—so the story is told—that for once he would make a point of getting drunk; how well and with what effects he kept his word, the sequel showed.

What particularly distressed the writer of this editorial was not so much the death of the lad, but the behaviour of the dead man's friends:

We believe that the companions of the young man (who were also driving carts) stated on their oath at the inquest, that they themselves were sober at the time of the accident. Sober or otherwise, instead of hastening back to Oswestry (from which they were only a few hundred yards distant) for medical assistance, they actually laid the still breathing form of their miserable companion across the shafts, as if it had been a sack of hay or corn, and so proceeded deliberately homewards. Let those who will, believe that sober men could have acted in this way. For our own part, for the credit of humanity and of the men themselves, we prefer, in despite of their own testimony, to believe that they were not in a condition to know what they were about.

January, 1855

In keeping with the non-conformist beliefs of its publisher, the Advertiser campaigned strongly against drinking on a Sunday:

The recent Act of Parliament for limiting the hours during which places of public refreshment may be kept open on Sundays, has been attended with excellent results. What is now proposed, is to carry it a step further and to obtain a law by which inns and public houses could be closed during the

A cover from November 1855

whole of Sunday, except to persons who have been travelling, and who are actually on a journey.

But its main concern was drunkenness:

It is only at a distance, and on the outside, that habits of drinking have anything attractive about them. Those who have beheld strong constitutions shattered, and fine minds destroyed, by excesses which began in nothing but "a friendly glass;" those who have witnessed the tears and humiliation of the wife, and the retributive ruin of the children, of the man who tries to imagine that he is "nobody's enemy but his own;"—those who have seen drinking habits on *this* side, which is their inner, and their true side, must have strange hearts indeed, if they are not willing to consent to the putting of some check to this cruel self abasement, and this curse to family peace.
March, 1855

It was not just the young who were treated with severity. Note the sentence this 87-year-old woman received for shoplifting. Hard labour usually meant the treadmill for several hours a day. It is said to have in effect killed Oscar Wilde, a much younger person:

A VETERAN IN CRIME.
Elizabeth Lewis, of Whittington, whose age was stated in the calendar at 87, was indicted for stealing one coat, the property of Mr John Whitridge Davies, tailor and draper, Church-street.— On the day in question the prisoner called at prosecutor's shop, and asked if a parcel had been left there for Mrs Ward, of Whittington, and was informed by prosecutor's brother that no such parcel had been left; the prisoner said she would wait until that lady came, and was then asked by the young man to step into the shop. This the prisoner declined to do, loitered about the doorway under pretence that she momentarily expected the arrival of her son.

When she left the shop a coat was missing. It was later found in her house by a police officer.

The prisoner avowed that she had picked the coat from off the streets, without knowing to whom it belonged, and called God as witness to the truth of her story.—The jury convicted the prisoner, and the Recorder, after enumerating a long list of offences of which she had previously been found guilty, sentenced her to 12 months' imprisonment, with hard labour.
April, 1855

The churchyard referred to here is of St Oswald's Church, known as the Old Church:

We would not wish to see our churchyard "cribbed, cabin and confined" with iron palisadings like to some of the yards in Birmingham and London, but would certainly prefer a plan similar to the one where it was suggested, that "the churchyard, so far as it is fully tenanted, (and that it is well nigh so all must admit) be planted with Evergreen, so as carefully to preserve sacred every grave and gravestone, and lend such garniture as

Nature herself can alone supply them with. We would lightly fence out the walks from the burial ground, not with a fence *seeming* even to forbid the visits of the living, but with one so light as to whisper "Come and welcome, but tread softly and with reverence."
May, 1855

This announcement was of huge importance to the Advertiser. The Newspaper Stamp Bill meant that at last news and other items could be printed without stamp duty being charged. When the Bill was passed, the first weekly edition of the Advertiser was published, on September 12, 1855:

In another column will be found an advertisement announcing the more frequent publication of the Oswestry Advertiser. The Newspaper Stamp Bill has passed the House of Commons, and been twice read in the Lords, but until it has received the Royal assent, we are not in a position to announce when our weekly series will commence. From good authority we are led to believe that before the month is out the Bill will have become law, and, if so, we purpose commencing the ensuing half-year with a weekly paper.
June, 1855.

Oswestry felt it had been sidelined by the great railway boon of the 1840s. In the 1850s it was believed that none of the main companies were going to build any more lines to or through the town. If Oswestry was going to prosper, local people would have to build the railways themselves:

OSWESTRY, WELSHPOOL, AND NEWTOWN RAILWAY.–This bill came before the committee of the House of Commons. The case for the bill was opened by Serjeant Wrangham, who stated that it was a measure promoted by the inhabitants of the district, to supply that railway accommodation which it had been deprived by the contests of the two great railway companies in 1853, and their subsequent truce, binding them to make no new lines. Probably there never was a line brought before the House so unanimously supported by the landowners and inhabitants of the district.
July, 1855

Again a problem in the town was the number of brothels, but getting rid of them wasn't easy:

The Town Clerk said that much had been written in the papers about the nuisance that existed in Salop Road. It was not so easy to convict as they seemed to think. He suggested that if the Corporation thought they had sufficient grounds for an action, they should employ a solicitor to prosecute on behalf of the town, and, of course, pay him for his trouble. Mr Davies said it would be impossible to convict without actual evidence, and they could hardly expect any man to criminate himself. Mr Morris said if the nuisance was removed it would settle elsewhere, though that would be better than to have it so public as it was.
November 14, 1855

The Bellman was the town crier, but the Council may not have chosen the best man:

BELLMAN.—Mr Hill proposed that they should get a new bellman. The man who now filled the office was a disgrace to the town; he was continually so drunk that he did not know what he was about, and often proclaimed sales after they were over: he would then demand pay from his employers, and insult them if they did not satisfy these demands.

Mr Bickerton thought that there ought to be a trifling salary attached to the office, and then there would be a chance of getting a respectable man. The bellman was called a servant to the Corporation, but all they did to him was to lend him a Bell.

November 14, 1855

Fire was a frequent problem, especially since the only water supply was streams or wells:

FIRE.—On Friday night last a fire broke out in the workshops of Mr Richard Jones, hatter, Bailey-street. The engines were speedily on the spot, but such was the intensity of the frost that water could not very readily be procured. The neighbourhood was thrown into a state of alarm, as it was known that a great quantity of hay was lying in an adjoining building. The fire was fortunately subdued, but not before damage to the amount of some £50 was done to Mr Jones's stock, which we are sorry to say was not insured.

December 26, 1855

The December 1854 edition of Roberts's Miscellany, the magazine published free to all Advertiser subscribers.

The story of the railways continued, with the Oswestry and Newtown Railway being built, if very slowly, and news of another one connecting with that railway:

SHREWSBURY AND WELSHPOOL RAILWAY.

It is proposed to apply to Parliament for power to make a Railway, commencing by a junction with the authorised line of the Oswestry and Newtown Railway.
January 2, 1856

In this case of John Adams there seemed only circumstantial evidence to convict him:

STEALING WIRE.

John Adams, a nailor, in the employ of Mr Lacon, was committed for stealing wire, on the night of the 11th of November, from the fence of a field belonging to W. Ormsby Gore, MP. Although no one saw him commit the act, the chain of evidence was singularly complete. James Payne saw him the same morning loitering about the field. Thomas Lloyd, taking cows to the field the next morning, discovered the loss. P.C.George Smallman found a quantity of wire, of a similar description, on Adam's block. Edward Williams, gaoler, in searching Adams' house, took a coil of wire from his wife, who was trying to conceal and carry it away, and Mr Evans, police-superintendent, examined the fence, and brought away a piece of wire that remained attached to one of the posts, and found it to match exactly at the end with one of the coils found in the prisoner's house.

Whether John Adams was innocent or not, he certainly put up a stout defence. He told the magistrates:

"Gentlemen, I am innocent. It's only spite and malice has done this–to separate me from my dear wife and children. My wife told me that my oldest son had found the wire I had in my house–there was spite to put it in my child's way. Henry Jones, the butcher, which he's a son-in-law of Mrs Roberts; I beat him at words, and so he struck me. I bought the wire they found in the shop of Master Dale, at three halfpence a pound, and made sparabils [*a kind of nail*] at five pence a pound, like mice's teeth. Let's have it all put down. Don't send a fellow from his blood and bones to bad principles."

The new larger size 1856 Advertiser — though it was to grow even more by the end of the year. There were no mottos on the front, but a long list of the towns and villages covered by the paper.

Here the magistrates interposed, and told him they were not surprised at his beating any one with words, but they could see nothing in his speech worth recording.
January 9, 1856

Interesting terms for drunkenness are used here:

BYE LAWS.–A case was heard before our Mayor on Friday last, in which one Jane Rush was charged with being found in a beastly state of intoxication. The police stated that the woman was continually transgressing and the mayor inflicted a fine of 20s. or in default 21 days imprisonment. It would be well just now March fair is being held, for those who get "jolly" on such occasions to remember that Magistrates have, under the Bye Laws power to fine heavily for the crime of drunkenness, and that they are disposed to exercise that power.
March 5, 1856

But drunkenness wasn't the only cause of trouble in Oswestry:

THE Oswestry Smithfield was, on Wednesday last, the scene of one of the most disgraceful riots it has ever been our lot to witness. Our readers are doubtless all aware that the question of the propriety of the Auctions in the Smithfield has been discussed on several occasions by the Town Council, and the results of these discussions has led to their sanctioning, under certain conditions, the continuance of the practice. There perhaps was never a subject discussed that could be so well supported with arguments on both sides.

On one side was Mr Hilditch, the auctioneer, and a member of the Town Council for many years, and his friends, who believed that a man had a right to sell his wares to the best advantage; and on the other side the dealers who reckoned that the introduction of auctions allowed false biddings to run up the price to a greater amount than they wanted to pay:

The riot we referred to was caused by some fifty or sixty of the dealers, who on the night before the fair entered into a conspiracy to upset the auction; but not content with merely entering their protests, and declining to bid, they chose to yell, hoot, and attempt to stop the proceedings. However in Mr Hilditch they met with their match, and whether he sold or not, he put up all the lots and fairly beat the opposition.
April 9, 1856

Unusual weather was frequently reported:

STORM OF HAIL.–On Friday last our town was visited by terrific storm of hail, accompanied by thunder and lightning. The streets at half-past twelve o'clock were two inches deep in hail.
May 28, 1856

In this court report, subtitled 'A Rum Case', John Davies, a carrier from Llanfyllin, tried to recover the sum of £2 17s 6d from David Edwards, who lived at Clawdd-du in Oswestry, for the value of a jar of rum Edwards had broken:

John Davies said–David Edwards carries goods about Oswestry in a hand-cart. I engaged him to carry half a barrel of porter and a jar of rum from the Station to the Bell Inn. He has often carried goods for me before.

Mr Henry Davies contended that the defendant was not a common carrier, and in breaking the jar it was not proved that gross negligence had been used.

His Honour–He was hired to carry, and if a man engages to carry other people's goods he is answerable for them. Judgement for plaintiff.

When the case was over, David Edwards said–"Your Honour, if I had known then what I know now, I'd have drunk some of that rum out of the channel!"

June 18, 1856

The sentence given in the next case seems on the surface to be extremely harsh; the girl's story is certainly very sad, and the behaviour of her mother terrible:

THE BEAR CORNER.

Sarah Rogers, one of the unfortunate girls living under the walls, pleaded guilty to stealing shillings from the person of Edward Davies.

Mr Henry Davies said–I am instructed in this case to state that the poor girl at the bar was, up to the age of 14, living in an excellent situation, from which she was beguiled under the pretence that her mother was very ill. Some wicked people, older than herself, took her to her mother, who, I am sorry to say, sanctioned their conduct, and the girl has been living in debauchery ever since. I have to ask whether your worship has not the power to send this poor girl to some reformatory, where she may be removed from her wicked courses.

His Worship said he had no power to send the girl to a reformatory, but he could pass upon her a heavy sentence, and applied to her Majesty's advisers to have her removed to some institution of the kind, and addressing the prisoner, said–Those who have brought you to your present state have a most heavy responsibility resting upon them. That a mother should be the cause of her daughter's ruin, body and soul, is dreadful to think of. The heavy penalty I am about to inflict, will, I hope, be the means of reclaiming you from the wicked course of life you have been trained in. The sentence of the court is that you be transported for 14 years, and I will endeavour that you be sent to some place where an opportunity will be given to you to amend.

This is the Advertiser's comment, and explanation for the girl's sentence of being transported for 14 years; it meant that there was some chance of rehabilitation for her:

The sentence of fourteen years' transportation for the first offence of robbery from the person would to any indifferent party appear a cruelly severe and unheard-of punishment. But in the case at our Sessions on Saturday last, had the Recorder sent the girl for three, six, or twelve months to gaol, she would have returned in all probability a hardened criminal; he had not the power to send her to a Penitentiary, but he could sentence her for a long term, and he will be able by representing her case to the higher powers to get her sent to some Reformatory. When placed in such an institution the length of her sentence will depend upon her conduct, and she may yet have occasion to be thankful to a kind judge who has removed her from the pernicious influence of her unnatural parent.

July 2, 1856

Three months later, the case was reported again, and the sentence seemed to have had the desired effect:

The Recorder, Mr J. R. Kenyon states that he has been to Shrewsbury gaol to visit Sarah Rogers, the girl whom readers will remember he sentenced to fourteen years' transportation. The governor and chaplain gave him a very good report of the girl's conduct; and she had been told that orders had been received for her removal. She was asked (as is usual) whether she wished to see any of her relatives before she was removed. She, however, said that she had no wish to see any of them. When the recorder asked her if she would not like to write to her grandmother, she burst out crying and seemed to shrink from writing to her. In the second letter, dated August 18, Mr Kenyon states that he has heard from the Secretary of State to the effect that Sarah Rogers will be placed in a refuge for the destitute, with a conditional *pardon*.

September 3, 1856

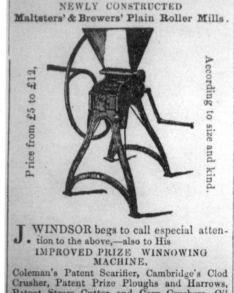

NEWLY CONSTRUCTED
Maltsters' & Brewers' Plain Roller Mills.

Price from £5 to £12,

According to size and kind.

J. WINDSOR begs to call especial attention to the above,—also to His
IMPROVED PRIZE WINNOWING MACHINE,
Coleman's Patent Scarifier, Cambridge's Clod Crusher, Patent Prize Ploughs and Harrows, Patent Straw Cutter and Corn Crushers, Oil Cake Breakers, Parkes's Cast Steel Digging Forks, and a variety of useful agricultural implements.

Agent for Clayton, Shuttleworth and Co's Patent Steam Engine and portable Thrashing Machines; for Milner's strong Holdfast and fire-resisting Safes; for the United Kingdom Temperance and General Provident Life and Fire Assurance Society, Head Office, 1, Adelaide Place, London Bridge; and for the Provincial (Welsh) Fire and Life Insurance Company.

Beatrice Street, Oswestry, Oct., 1855.

This is an extreme case of animal cruelty:

CRUELTY TO ANIMALS.–An act of unwonted cruelty was practised by some abandoned wretches, on Sunday night last, upon a donkey, belonging to Messrs. Morris, builders. The poor animal was discovered with its ears and tail torn off as with a knife or saw! A reward of £25 has been offered to any party who will give information of the offender, and we sincerely trust that it may be the means of bringing the perpetrator to justice.
July 2, 1856

Illnesses such as typhus and cholera, caused by polluted water, were common:

OUR SANITARY CONDITION.–At the meeting of the burial committee on Monday, Mr Longueville remembered the case of typhus, in Upper Brook Street, had recently come under his notice. That street ought to be the most healthy in the town, but he had observed that invariably typhus fever commenced there; and he asked whether the drainage was not imperfect? The Mayor said he had long been of opinion, that we ought to have a public meeting of the inhabitants to consider our sanitary condition.
July 23, 1856

Begging was treated harshly:

John Hill, Charles Turner, George Lewis, John Atkins (dry-land sailors), had been taken into custody by P.C. Jones for begging, and two of them for exposing sores on their bodies, for the purpose of exciting commiseration. Committed to the house of correction: Atkins for six weeks, Hill for five weeks, and the other two for one month each.
July 30, 1856

There are frequent reports of illegitimate babies dying at birth after the girl kept her pregnancy a secret, the death caused either as there was no medical treatment, or because the mother disposed of the baby. This is a typical example:

INQUEST AT OSWESTRY.
An inquest was held at the Bear Inn, Oswestry, yesterday afternoon, on the body of a male infant, and the following evidence was heard. On Saturday last Mary Jones, the daughter of John Jones, slater, was very unwell, and continued so until yesterday, when she advised the father to have medical advice. Dr Fuller was sent for, and on examining the girl said that she had been delivered of a child, and asked where it was. The girl admitted it, and said she had buried the infant in the privy. On searching, the body was found and taken up by Philip Windsor with a sharavel [a shovel, possibly?] which he bent for the purpose. He had considerable difficulty in getting the body out. Dr Fuller (who had made a post-mortem examination at the request of the jury) said, that the child must have lived half an hour or more, after birth, from the almost perfect inflation of both lungs. The jury gave in the following verdict–"we find that the child was born alive, but we

have no evidence as to how it came by its death."
July 30, 1856

This follows on from the November 1855 report about the drunken bellman – but the solution to his conduct was clearly in his clothes:

OSWESTRY TOWN COUNCIL.–BELLMAN.
It having been announced that Frank Syer, the bellman, had sent in his resignation, Mr Saunders proposed and Mr Bickerton seconded that the late bellman, Davies, should be reappointed.
Mr Minshall lamented that a sober, steady man could not be obtained for the office; he feared there was something vagrant in the employment, or they would have been more successful in obtaining a man.
Mr Bickerton said that if they wanted a really good man, they must give a good salary. The office was not worth more than 3s. a week.
Mr Rogers observed that if the old bellman was reappointed, he would suggest that they should dress him in a red suit again. He had not been the same man since they had dressed him in blue!
August 13, 1856

The Maesbury Road was and is a dangerous place, though perhaps not in the same way as now. Unusually, drink is not involved:

ANOTHER FATAL ACCIDENT ON THE MAESBURY ROAD.
An inquest was held on Saturday last, at the Ball Inn, Maesbury, on the body of David Jones, a lad of 17 years of age, who was found lying dead on the road, a few hundred yards from the Mile Oak Gate, on the afternoon of the day previous. The deceased had been to Oswestry for some lead piping. He was seen by Mary Meredith going through the turnpike gate soon after three o'clock, and at that time was sitting in the cart with the reins in his hand. It is supposed that he was dozing when the accident occurred, having been up late the night previous finishing the harvest. Richard Jones found the poor fellow on the road quite dead, with a mark, as of a wheel, across his head. The horse and cart were nowhere near at that time. A verdict of "accidental death" was returned. This is the third fatal accident that has occurred on the Maesbury Road within the last two years, but on this occasion, we are glad to say, the victim was not guilty of the crime of drunkenness or riding on the shafts, the usual causes of such accidents.
September 3, 1856

It seems rather unfair that this case was reported with such hilarity:

A HARD CASE.–As one Edward Jones, of Sweeney, was returning from the Old Church last Monday morning, having just been "launched into matrimony," he was welcomed on his way home by P.C.Thomas Jones, and apprehended on a charge of felony! He is remanded until Thursday, when the case will be gone into and decided whether he shall spend his

honeymoon on the banks of the Severn at Shrewsbury or on the mountain at Sweeney.
October 1, 1856

This is taken from a review of *The Castle of Oswestry*, by James Blake. It suggests that the Castle Bank was, or should have been, the town's most important tourist site:

The tourist, traveller, or casual visitor, who has read the history of England, or the more immediate history of the conquest of the Britons and eventful wars of the Welsh; on entering Oswestry, in vain looks for any monument to commemorate the important part the town has shared in those disastrous and turbulent commotions. It is needless to review the very many notorious and highly interesting incidents which, in the history of this country from the earliest times, has marked this town and its citadel with such interest to the antiquarian, historian, or general reader; and we cannot be surprised that on any of these coming into the town his first enquiry would be for the remains of this ancient fortification.
October 15, 1856

Now the Advertiser was expanding into Wales, and changing its name:

PROPOSED ENLARGEMENT AND OTHER ALTERATIONS.
THE OSWESTRY ADVERTISER, MONTGOMERYSHIRE MERCURY, AND Local Journal for the Borders of Wales
Eight years ago the Oswestry Advertiser was commenced as a Small Monthly Sheet, almost solely for the purpose of publishing the Time Tables of the Shrewsbury and Chester Railway, and by the publication of a few advertisements making known the wants of the advertising gentlemen of Oswestry.

The Proprietor is grateful for the confidence which the public has placed in him. He has accordingly purchased a printing machine, constructed after the newest model, and with the most recent improvements, by which he can issue a *thousand sheets in an hour*. He confidently expects that he will thus be able to make the paper a thoroughly efficient local organ, and looks forward as the result to a weekly circulation of a least *five thousand copies*.

During the last few months the paper has especially

THE BORDERS OF WALES!
WITH the commencement of 1857 will be issued a New and ENLARGED Series of the *Advertiser* under the title of the
OSWESTRY ADVERTISER.
MONTGOMERYSHIRE MERCURY
And Local Journal for the Borders of Wales.
Agents and Correspondents will be appointed in several towns and villages in the Border Counties, and the paper will be printed with a POWERFUL MACHINE, erected specially, capable of working off a *thousand impressions an hour*.
☞ The Price will be the same as heretofore, ONE PENNY, and the paper will contain a mass of LOCAL NEWS connected with Shropshire, Montgomeryshire, and other neighbouring counties, not to be found in any other paper.

OSWESTRY ADVERTISER,

MONTGOMERYSHIRE MERCURY

And Local Journal for the Borders of Wales.

Printed with one of

MYERS'S CAXTON MACHINES

The new machine bought to print the Advertiser

increased in its circulation through a proportion of Montgomeryshire, a county that has no newspaper published in any of its towns, and which is very inadequately represented by any existing journal. When the railway is taken from Oswestry to Newtown, Oswestry will be, more than at present, the connecting link between England and Montgomeryshire, so he intends devoting a considerable portion of his space to the events transpired in that county.
October 15, 1856

This report of a fire in a shop seems at first to be nothing out of the ordinary, except for the barber bursting into the chapel in the middle of a service:

SUSPICIOUS FIRE.–On Sunday night last, about seven o'clock, an alarm of fire was given, when it was discovered that the shop called the "Bee Hive," situated in Church-street, in the occupation of Mr Andrew Jones, draper and grocer, was on fire. The engines were speedily on the spot, but fortunately their services were not required, as the prompt measures adopted had subdued the flames. The circumstances connected with this fire are very suspicious:–it appears that Mr Jones and his family had gone into the country on Sunday morning, and had left the house with no one in it. About seven o'clock in the evening, Mr Charles Thomas, of the Fox Inn, was standing at the door of his house, observed a glare through the fanlight of Mr Jones's shop and called to George Edwards, barber, who was at the door of his shop, to come and look. Edwards burst the door, and an alarm was given. Mr Donald was speedily on the premises, and the fire was extinguished. Edwards, with more zeal than discretion, ran up to the primitive Methodist Chapel, where Jones is in the habit of attending, and disturbed the congregation by shouting out that his shop was on fire, speedily clearing the chapel by his information.

But clearly there had been some foul play — and there is a very strong hint in the final sentence about who might have been responsible:

From the particulars we have been able to learn (but which it would at present be premature to publish) there can be no doubt but that this fire was the work of an incendiary, as candles, nearly burnt out, were found placed in bonnet boxes in two separate places in the shop; a lighted candle was also found on the kitchen table. Who the scoundrel is who planned this diabolical scheme, we know not, but we trust the clue will speedily be found, and that he will be brought to justice. Strange to say, Mr Jones only insured his stock a week or two back!

November 26, 1856

This gives an idea of the kind of cases that came before the Oswestry magistrates in a typical month:

Superintendent Evans, of the A. division, read to the magistrates a list of cases which had come under his notice during the month of October last, a large proportion of which he said proceeded from drunkenness. The number amounted to 65, as follows–1 beerhouse information, 13 drunkenness, 18 breach of the peace, 5 riding without reins, 1 hawking without license, 2 vagrancy, 4 unjust weights and measures, 1 pound case, 7 assault, 1 want of sureties, 3 trespassing in pursuit of game, 2 bastardy, 5 felony, 1 receiving stolen goods, 1 assault with intent.

December 3, 1856

It was necessary to have good eyesight or a strong magnifying glass when reading the Advertiser. This is a lifesize copy of a letter printed in the November 14, 1855, edition.

Letter to the Editor.

THE CHURCH.

Sir,—In a former number of the OSWESTRY ADVERTISER a few remarks appeared proving the illegality of selling, buying, or letting pews in a Parish Church. The attention of those who feel any interest in seeing a better system introduced, is requested while we endeavour to shew the sinfulness of the Pew System, and the extent of the evils arising from it; and in order to see fully how very far we have strayed from the "old paths" in this particular, we have but to make ourselves acquainted with what has always been acknowledged as the right principle since the time of the Apostles.

"The poor have the Gospel preached to them," said our Lord, and from among the poor He called those whom He made His friends on earth, and upon whom He conferred the high honour of the Apostleship. Ever since that time, when the Church of Christ was emphatically declared to be the Church of the Poor, have Churches been places where all have an equal right to worship the great Head of the Church, no matter what may be their condition of life, for "God is no respecter of persons." This has always been the undeniable theory of the Church. The Church of England, as the National Church, belongs to the whole people, and the law of the land, and the 15th Canon of the Church enact that every Englishman is entitled to be duly and regularly accommodated in the Church of the place where he lives.

Let not then the poor imagine that it is the Church that excludes them, or that prevents their worshipping within her sacred walls. So far from doing so, she mourns over the

The editor of the Advertiser moved his home and printing works to a house on Beatrice Street he called Caxton House. The Advertiser was now called 'The Oswestry Advertiser, Montgomeryshire Mercury, and Local Journal for the Borders of Wales':

> The first number of our new series, which we now present to the public, although it is not altogether so good as we could have wished it, is still a fair sample of what we intend to do in future. Our sheet is not quite so large as some of our friends expected to see it, we know; but they must remember that our price is unchanged, and what can they expect for a Penny! We gave twenty closely-printed columns, of which nearly fourteen are composed of News as well-condensed and interesting as we ourselves and our correspondents (most of them specially appointed), can make it.
>
> *January 7, 1857*

After seven years of waiting, at last it seemed that progress was being made on building the new Oswestry and Newtown railway (the 'Welshpool' had been quietly dropped from the title):

> We are much gratified to hear from several sources that the land valuers are actually engaged in purchasing the land for this line, and that foremost amongst those who have shown their anxiety to second the efforts of this company to introduce railway accommodation into Central Wales, by promptly selling their lands on fair terms, we find the name of David Pugh, Esq., MP, for the Montgomeryshire Borough, whose lands extend, we hear, over nearly three miles of the land.
>
> *January 14, 1857*

But only a month later the Advertiser was doubtful that anything would ever happen:

> OSWESTRY AND NEWTOWN RAILWAY.
>
> The many different times that those in authority have led us to expect that the "first sod" was about to be turned, leaves it, we fear, beyond doubt that some secret influences are at work to cause the vexatious delays which have occurred.
>
> We may remind our readers, that some time ago a committee was appointed to watch the proceedings of Railway Companies in connection with our town. What is that committee doing? Assuredly, if there ever was a time when watchfulness was necessary, that time is *now*.
>
> *February 18, 1857*

Frequently these days a letter or comment in the Advertizer will question why some road or other was dug up, or why the streets are poorly lit. This is nothing new, but here the letter writer tries to excuse those responsible:

> DEAR SIR,–In the last week's *Advertiser* you state that a correspondent under the elegant signature of "Stick-in-the-Mud" asks two questions,–1st, "Why the streets of Oswestry are left so long unpaved after the gasmen had broken them up?" 2nd, "Why the town was not lit up with gas on Monday

GREAT WESTERN RAILWAYS TABLE FOR OCT.

London, Birmingham, Wolverhampton, Shrewsbury, Chester, Birkenhead, & Liverpool.

Mr. J. L. FISHER, Station Master and Goods Agent at Oswestry.

UP TRAINS.

LEAVE	I. 1 & 2	II. 1,2,3	III. 1 & 2	IV. 1 & 2	V. 1 & 2	VI. 1 & 2	VII. 1 & 2	VIII. 1 & 2	IX. 1 & 2	X. 1,2,3	XI. 1 & 2	SUNDAYS 1,2,3
LIVERPOOL		8 20	9 0	10 30		1 15	1 30	3 35	4 15	6 30	8 30	4 20
Birkenhead		8 35	9 15	10 45		1 30	1 45	3 55	4 30	6 45	8 50	4 35
CHESTER Arr.		8 10	9 10	10 10	11 15	2 0		3 21	4 15	5 20	7 45	9 50 / 5 10
CHESTER Dep.		8 20						3 21		5 26		9 56 / 5 16
Saltney		8 20										
Pulford												
Rossett		8 33		10 23				3 33		5 38	7 58	10 11 / 5 31
Gresford		8 42		10 29				3 42		5 47	8 7	10 18 / 5 38
Wrexham		8 53	9 35	10 36	11 38	2 25		3 53	4 40	5 58	8 18	10 29 / 5 49
Ruabon		9 7		10 47	11 50			4 7	4 52	6 12	8 31	10 44 / 6 4
Cefn		9 13		10 53				4 14		6 18		10 50 / 6 10
Llangollen Road (1)		9 18		10 58	11 57			4 20		6 23	8 39	10 55 / 6 15
Chirk		9 23		11 3	12 2	2 45		4 26	5 2	6 28	8 44	10 59 / 6 19
Gobowen (2)		9 33	10 0	11 13	12 13	2 55		4 37	5 12	6 38	8 55	11 8 / 6 28
OSWESTRY Dep.		9 23	9 50	11 0	12 0	2 45		4 25	5 0	6 28	8 45	10 58 / 6 15
OSWESTRY Arr.		9 43	10 10	11 23	12 23	3 10		4 47	5 23	6 48	9 5	11 18 / 6 38
Whittington (2)		9 38		11 18				4 44		6 45	9 2	11 13 / 6 33
Rednal (4)		9 46		11 26			3 8	4 51		6 52	9 13	11 19 / 6 39
Baschurch		9 58		11 38		2 20		5 5		7 3	9 25	11 32 / 6 52
Leaton		10 5		11 45				5 13		7 10		11 40 / 7 0
SHREWSBURY Arr.		10 20	10 30	11 55	12 45	3 35		5 30	5 38	7 25	9 40	11 50 / 7 10
SHREWSBURY Dep.	8 0	10 40	10 35	12 0	12 55	3 40		5 45		7 35		11 55 / 7 15
Wellington	8 22	11 9	10 53	12 22	1 15	4 8		6 5	8 1		12 15	7 45
Shiffnal	8 43	11 30	11 10	12 41		4 29		6 22	8 22		12 35	8 10
W'hampton Arr.	9 16	12 10	11 33	1 18	1 50	5 5		6 45	9 0		1 5	8 45
W'hampton Dep.	9 18	12 15	11 35	1 20	1 53	3 25	5 10	6 47	9 5		1 10	8 55
Birmingham Arr.	9 40	1 0	12 0	2 5	2 20	4 5	5 35	7 10	9 50		1 55	9 45
Birmingham Dep.	9 45	1 5	12 10	2 30	2 30	4 10	5 40	7 15			2 5	
Leamington	10 23	2 0	12 45	3 0	3 0	5 6	6 33	7 48			2 46	
Oxford	11 55	3 45	1 55	4 5	4 5	8 15	8 43				3 55	
Reading	12 55	4 45	2 52	4 45	4 45	9 30					5 6	
LONDON Arr.	2 25	5 40	3 50	5 40	5 40	10 35					6 40	

DOWN TRAINS.

LEAVE	1,2,3	1 & 2	1 & 2	Exp.	1 & 2	1,2,3	1 & 2	1 & 2	Exp.	1,2,3 fr. slp
LONDON				6 0	9 15		7 30	11 0	2 0	4 50 / 9 0
Reading				7 10	10 2		9 10	12 3	3 0	5 37 / 10 25
Oxford				8 20	10 48		10 55	1 5	3 45	6 27 / 11 45
Leamington			8 0	10 2	11 44		12 45	2 18	4 57	7 20 / 1 30
Birmingham Arr.			8 50	10 45	12 15		1 50	3 0	5 40	8 0 / 2 30
Birmingham Dep.	6 0		8 55	10 55	12 25		2 0	3 10	5 50	8 10 / 7 15 / 2 40
W'hampton Ar.	6 40		9 20	11 30	12 50		2 50	3 45	6 18	8 38 / 8 0 / 3 13
W'hampton Dep.	6 45		9 22	11 32	12 52		2 55	3 50	6 20	8 40 / 8 5 / 3 21
Shiffnal	7 18		9 53	12 6			3 35	4 20	6 55	9 5 / 8 37 / 3 57
Wellington	7 42		10 15	12 27	1 27		3 58	4 36	7 15	9 20 / 8 58 / 4 17
SHREWSBURY Arr.	7 0	8 10	10 30	12 45	1 45		4 25	4 55	7 33	9 38 / 9 20 / 4 40
SHREWSBURY Dep.	7 10	8 15	10 35	12 50	1 47		4 40	5 0	7 35	9 40 / 9 25 / 4 45
Leaton	7 10						4 50			9 35 / 4 55
Baschurch (5)	7 20	8 30		1 8			5 0	5 20	7 50	9 45 / 5 6
Rednal (4)	7 32			1 20			5 12		8 2	9 57 / 5 20
Whittington (3)	7 42			1 27			5 22			10 5 / 5 29
Gobowen (2)	7 52	8 52	11 10	1 35	2 22		5 45	5 40	8 16	10 10 / 10 13 / 5 35
OSWESTRY Dep.	8 0	8 40	11 0	1 25	2 12		5 28	5 25	3 5	10 10 / 10 20 / 5 25
OSWESTRY Arr.	8 2	9 2	11 23	1 45	2 35		5 50	5 50	3 25	10 20 / 10 23 / 5 45
Chirk	8 0	8 40	11 16	1 42					3 22	10 14 / 10 20 / 5 46
Llangollen Road (1)	8 6	9 5	11 20	1 47					3 26	10 26 / 5 52
Cefn	8 11									10 30 / 5 56
Ruabon	8 20	9 15	11 30	1 55	2 40				8 36	10 37 / 6 3
Wrexham	8 32	9 27	11 42	2 8	2 52				8 48	10 32 / 10 43 / 6 18
Gresford	8 39	9 33		2 16						10 55 / 6 27
Rossett	8 44	9 37		2 20						11 0 / 6 32
Pulford										
Saltney	8 55									11 10 / 6 40
CHESTER Arr.	9 5	9 50	12 5	2 38	3 0		6 30	6 30	9 10	11 10 / 6 46
CHESTER Dep.	9 10	10 0	12 10	2 45	3 10		6 35	6 35	9 15	11 5 / 11 25 / 6 55
Birkenhead	9 45	10 40	12 40	3 5	3 35		7 0	7 0	10 0	11 30 / 11 45 / 7 50
LIVERPOOL	10 0	10 55	12 45	3 50	3 50		7 15	7 15	10 15	11 45 / 12 10 / 9 5

1. Station for Llangollen, Corwen, &c. 2. near Martins and Selattyn. 3. Ellesmere. 4. West Felton, Knockin, Kinnerley. 5. Wem. The Junction for Oswestry is at Gobowen. * Third Class to & from all stations between Oswestry and Chester. W Wednesday. T Thursday.

When the Advertiser started it printed the railway timetables every month, but by 1857 they were printed just once a year. In 1857 it took almost five hours to reach London from Gobowen by train – and over 30 hours by stage coach. The fastest scheduled time by train now is under three hours.

night?" The first of these questions you answer by saying, that you "don't know;" and the second, "because the night was very dark!"

As regards the first query, I believe the true answer to it is between the gas proprietor and the paviour [*the person who paves the streets*]. In reference to the second question, Mr Roberts by his contract for lighting the town is allowed four nights in each moon that the lamps are not lit–two nights before the full, the night of the full, and the night after.

Yours truly, A LOOKER-ON

(Our Correspondent will perhaps be surprised when we tell him that *Stick-in-the-Mud*, who propounded the questions he now answers, is an "elegant" young lady, and one of his acquaintance, so he had better be cautious how he finds fault with the signature she chooses to adopt!)

February 18, 1857

The answer to the letter came the following week:

SIR,–Will you permit me through the medium of your valuable columns to ask "A Looker on" why the lamps are put out long before it is daylight, as was the case on Sunday morning last, when they were out before 5 o'clock. As he seems acquainted with the terms of the contract, perhaps he can inform me if there is any specified hour for putting out the lights, or is it left to the discretion of the lamplighter.

I am, Sir, yours &c., AN EARLY RISER.

(We have never seen "the bond" *Looker on* referred to, so we cannot answer our correspondent's question. One thing we should like to know, and that is what an *Early Riser* wanted out of his bed so early on Sunday morning!)

March 4, 1857

The following letter is written entirely in Oswestry dialect, and provides an interesting comparison to today, with its 'wunna' and 'Odgestry'. It does express a common fear, that the Oswestry and Newtown Railway would never be built, and the shareholders would all lose their money:

ODGESTRY AND NEWTOWN RALEWAY.

MISTER HEDDITUR,–In yore papur last wick, yo sed summat about the Odgestry and Newtown raleway, and as i sid my ould feyther riting a letter, I should like to tell yo how the ould fellers' grubbed about the goin on o things; fust place then the ould lad as got aumost too thowsand in the Haffair (better he had spent some on it on my larning), well the ould boy thinks as how the hingeneres, and kontracters, and them parliament chaps and law men, will gollop up all the munney, and keep all the hoysters to themsels and poor sharehouders wunna get so much as a shel. now Mister Hedditur i tell yo wod i think them Direckters aut to do and not umbug folks like they am; well then in the fust place if there hinna a strateforrard hundderstanding at the next meteing and the kontracts all sined, and the day settled for cutting the fust clod and every thing cerene and comfortable then I say let them as got munney in the haffair like our ould chap rise up in a lump, and tell them direckters that they am to be umbugged no longer in this jacky lantern way.

I am, Mister Hedditur, MY FEYTHUR'S SUN JIM

April 8, 1857

This correspondent, who seems to have twelve children, complains about the church tax (apparently compulsory) called Easter Dues, and makes a pointed remark about the vicar usually being absent from the town:

EASTER "DOOS."

MR EDITOR,–I have been called upon during the past week to pay what are termed "Easter Dues"–a small amount certainly, but still a sum that I would have preferred spending in some other way. I want to know why I must pay Fourpence per Annum to the Vicar for the right of trading in Oswestry? I have plenty of expenses in the shape of rent, gas, poor's-rates, highway-rate, income-tax, and a variety of other matters "too numerous to mention," and fancy the Vicar might content himself with his church-rates. And why should the Vicar want Twopence per annum from each of my children? Poor little dears, they would rather spend the money in cake shops–all the twelve of them!

It is a long time since our worthy Shepherd has visited his flock; let me suggest that he be invited to come over on the next occasion and collect these "doos" himself, and I don't fancy we shall ever again be asked for the payment of them.

I am, Mr Editor, yours truly, PATERFAMILIAS

May 20, 1857

This would seem a strange complaint, until we read about what is behind it – drink, again:

Bell ringing in Oswestry has become a perfect nuisance, and on the slightest pretext the men are at the ropes, not for the purpose of doing honour to any particular person, but for the sake of getting supplied with drink, and it is high time the churchwardens exercised their right (for we presume they have

ON board H.M. Ship, *Assistance*, in the Arctic Regions, such was the superior performance of one of Jones's Levers above those of other makers, that it was agreed among Thirty of the Ship's company, on their return, to purchase each a Watch at the manufactory, 338, Strand, (opposite Somerset House.)

On Board H. M. Ship "North Star," in the Arctic Regions, for two years the ship's time was kept by one of JONES' LEVERS, all other watches on board having stopped.

Silver Levers, £4 4s.; Gold, £10 10s.; variation warranted not to exceed one minute per week under uniform conditions. Read Jones's "Sketch of Watch Work," free for a 2d. stamp.

On receipt of a Post Office Order for 1s. above the price of the Watch, addressed to JOHN JONES, 338, Strand, one will be sent free to any part of the Kingdom.

a right?) in the supervision of the bells. We have heard more than one complaint from respectable inhabitants of Church Street on the matter.
May 20, 1857

This is a variation on an old trick. The victim was 'of course a female':

FORTUNE-TELLING–On Thursday last a wandering Zingari improved her finances by means of the oft told plan of telling a fortune. The victim–of course a female–was a servant residing not hundred miles from "Salop Road," and with that unbounded curiosity, so peculiar to the sex, was ready to invoke the supernatural in any shape could she but know "the colour of his hair, when they would be wed, what the results would be–and the like." The terms were easy, the stars were not to be pressed into the service, incantations were not to be used, indeed, even the lines on the hand were not to be examined! The case was simple; all the money the girl had was to be wrapped (by the gypsy) in a handkerchief; this was to be laid under the girl's pillow at night; dreams were insured by this (very) simple process, and the next morning a young woman would have had curiosity amply satisfied. Three sovereigns were produced, the gipsy carefully folded the handkerchief, the young woman placed it under the pillow, what she dreamed we are not informed, but what she found when she examined the handkerchief next morning was three coins, made of what the gypsy undoubtedly had plenty stock of, viz.–*brass*!
May 20, 1857

This is an excerpt from a long letter, a forceful and eloquent protest against philandering men:

What has the peasant boy been guilty of, who is undergoing imprisonment with hard labour? He was caught with a net, in which he had one night snared a rabbit. What has that pale man in prison dress done, whom they are whipping in gaol? He stole a loaf, and deems his sentence merciful that he has not been transported. Ask that servant in the hulks why he is there? What has he done? He stole sixpence from his master's till.

But look at THAT man! He has seduced the daughter of his neighbour, of his tradesman, perhaps of his tenants, or of his friend. He has ruined for this life, if not for an eternal one, that once guileless and virtuous girl. The once blushing and retiring one walks the streets a brazen wanton, seeking her bread (of which there was enough and to spare in her father's house) by the ruin of others, till an early grave closes over her worn-out and lothsome frame. And England has no law to restrain, to intimidate, to punish the execrable villain who laughs at her mother's tears, at a father's silent agony, and defies the maddened brother to touch his law-protected person, for law, in her majesty, with her finger on her lips, looked on and smiles. Neither legislator nor magistrate utters a word, and the political economist says, with a shrug and a cold sardonic grin,

"She consented, and would you interfere with the freedom of the will?"
A JURIST
May 27, 1857

This is the first, but not last, appearance of Sloper, one of the characters of Oswestry:

STABBING.–At the Magistrates' Office, yesterday, a lad named Joseph Davies, *alias* Sloper, was charged with striking Thomas Jones, ostler at the White Lion, on the head with a knife. Jones has said that on Sunday night he was closing the gates in yard, when the lad struck at his fingers and hindered him closing it. At last complainant threw a stone at him, on which the lad went away, but waited for him with a knife, with which he inflicted a cut on his head. The magistrates dismissed the case, as the lad is but half witted.
June 3, 1857

The reply to the case came the following week:

SIR,–In your last paper I noticed that a half-witted boy was brought before the magistrates charged with stabbing a man in Willow-street, and the result of the examination was that the lad was discharged because he was not a responsible agent. Surely, then, something further will be done. It can never be the intention of the magistrates to allow a maniac to be loose on our streets? If such be the case, mischief will certainly be done.
Yours truly
June 10, 1857

There was yet another expansion of the Advertiser, to 17 by 22 inches, larger than any national paper printed now. This time the expansion had a price increase:

On the first day of July next will be issued a single sheet, full newspaper size, containing 24 column; and as it will be quite impossible to make this addition without raising the price, the charge in future will be Twopence per week.
June 10, 1857

This reports one of the common dangers of the time – though checking a gas leak with a candle was perhaps not the most sensible thing to do:

GAS EXPLOSION.–Soon after 11 o'clock on Friday night last an escape of gas was noticed by one of the lodgers at Mr Evans' (builder) Gibraltar House. Mr Evans very unadvisedly went upstairs with a candle in his hand followed by his wife; immediately they entered the room an explosion took place and they were both frightfully burnt. Two children were in bed in the room, who are also badly burnt about the arms. Mr Evans, we understand, had recently cut off the chandelier in the room but instead of getting the gasmen to stop the pipes properly had himself patched the mark with white lead and oil.
July 1, 1857

The following week there was a correction:

> Mr Evans has informed us that he had closed the pipe by hammering the lead together in such a manner as to render the escape of gas impossible. He also states that his object in cutting off the chandelier in question was to try and prevent the escape of gas by which the inmates of the house had been annoyed for a long time, and that he had repeatedly sent for the gasmen to come and attend to it.
> *July 8, 1857*

People seemed to think the Oswestry, Welshpool, and Newtown railway would never be built, but then came this important announcement:

> CUTTING THE FIRST SOD!
> It is now positively fixed that this long-looked for event will take place in the first week in August. The ceremony will take place near the Bowling Green, Welshpool, and it is supposed that Lady Williams Wynn will cut the first sod.
> *July 15, 1857*

Immediately after the first sod was cut, work began:

> OSWESTRY, WELSHPOOL, AND NEWTOWN RAILWAY. COMMENCEMENT OF THE WORKS. Our readers will be gratified to know that the works have actually commenced, and that on Monday last two waggon-loads of planks and barrows were conveyed from the Oswestry Railway Station to the Pant, where land has been engaged in the reception of the plant. In a few days we may expect an inundation of "Navvies," and confidently hope our prophecy will be fulfilled of seeing a railway to Llanymynech by Christmas!
> *August 12, 1857*

THE CELEBRATED
St. OSWALD'S WELL SODA AND POTASH WATER

EACH Bottle containing a due proportion of Alkali; also Aërated Lemonade of superior quality and manufactured with great care by Mr. W. Edwards, may now be obtained in the highest state of perfection, wholesale and retail, of

G. J. SAUNDERS,
Chemist, &c., Oswestry.

The reason Oswestry railway station was built at the far end of Beatrice Street, and not near Leg Street, was because the GWR was already there, and were unwilling to shift:

> A resolution of the Great Western Board

was read to the effect that the Station at Oswestry was to be placed as near as possible to the present one in order that the goods and passenger traffic may be under one management. They were willing to meet the wishes of the inhabitants of Oswestry provided an adequate share of the expenses was borne by the town.

The cost of making the Station in Leg-street would involve a much greater expense. The covering of the sewers (Mud Pits) would make it fully £1,000, for which they would not benefit one shilling per annum.

August 5, 1857

The Mud Pits were the open sewers, in Coney Green, where waste water went. They were a source of great annoyance:

THE MUD PITS.

At the Town Council meeting, Mr Alderman Cartwright commented upon the extreme nuisance of the Town Ditch in the Coney Green. Committee after committee had denounced it as a most disgraceful recruit to the town, that it had been allowed to endure so long a time. Recently Mr Cartwright had examined it, in consequence of arrangements being in progress as to the railway station to be erected near to that locality, and he must owe he had never examined a more pestiferous ditch; it was a hot day when he looked at it, there was scarcely a prill of water running through it; it was bankful of mud, and the exhalation from it was of the most offensive and dangerous character. Clearly, if the sewage of the town was allowed to run into the ditch, and pollute the atmosphere, the inhabitants were amenable

under the nuisance removal act to correct such an evil, and to cover over the ditch. He was truly ashamed to hear Mr Joseph Cubitt (the celebrated engineer) say that he had rarely ever seen so filthy a place allowed to exist so near the dwelling houses of a town.
August 12, 1857

A letter made a little ironic comment on the above:

SIR.–Can any of your readers inform my young folks, who lately passed through your ancient town on their return from the Cambrian Hills, who "ST MARY MUDDPITZ" was, and why she was canonised.
Your obedient servant, J.H.W.
September 2, 1857

This is the first appearance of the new superintendent of police, William Sykes. The house he went to seems a typical slum dwelling, but truly dreadful:

AN OSWESTRY LODGING HOUSE.
A few nights ago, Superintendent Sykes went into a house in Brook Street composed of two rooms and an attic, each of which were so small that the walls could be touched on either side by a man standing with outstretched arms in the centre, and found no less than 3 men, 10 women, and 2 dead bodies! There was not a chair nor a bed in the house, the stench from the place was abominable, and the whole of the furniture in the place, (if furniture it could be called), was not worth five shillings., Our impression is that Superintendent Sykes shapes now as he means to continue; and we look forward hopefully to a better regulation of lodging houses and beer shops.
November 4, 1857

Joseph Davies, alias Sloper, appears again:

ONE OF OUR JUVENILE ARABS.–Joseph Davies, alias Sloper, was charged with stealing some accordions out of the Market Hall. The circumstances were very peculiar, as prisoner was deaf and dumb. Robert Thomas was sworn to interpret, and by signs elicited that Davies said he did not steal the articles himself, but that Morgan went over for them. A plea of not guilty was therefore recorded. Morgan was a witness against prisoner, and Mr Charles Minshall (for the prosecution) put him into the box. He swore that prisoner had sold him one of the accordions and a knife; which, when interpreted to the prisoner, he denied, and intimated that it was just the other way–that Morgan had sold them to him. A verdict of guilty was returned, and Davies was sentenced to six weeks' imprisonment, after the expiration of which, he will be sent to a reformatory for five years.

December 30, 1857

The building of the Oswestry and Newtown Railway was going so slowly it had almost stopped. Superintendent Sykes received a bad press from one person:

WOMAN'S TONGUE.–Mary Williams from Land's End, was charged with being drunk and disorderly. She said she came into town the night before, and went to Mr Sykes's; Mr Sykes came out and "laid hold on her just as if she was a piece of dirt under his feet." She expressed her opinion that the "police ought to be reported to Victoria and Prince Albert," and asked the superintendent "how he dared put his hand nigh her." Mrs Williams concluded by observing that P.C.Williams had said to her that morning "come out you old faggot," and "was a faggot a proper name to give a grandmother and a woman sixty-nine years old." The Mayor kindly relieved the poor creature, who promised to go out of the town.
February 3, 1858

Though punishments such as the stocks and the pillory may seem medieval to us, the Advertiser campaigned strongly for their retention for certain crimes:

There are other ways of putting down the habit of drinking: petition the Houses of Parliament that the most absurd law, that fines a nobleman going home from his club, "slightly inebriated," *five shillings and costs*, be repealed, and that, instead of a money fine, every fellow, whether Lord or Commoner, who disgraces himself by getting drunk, be compelled to sit out his six hours, rain or sunshine, frost or snow, in the most public thoroughfare, in the good old English piece of parish furniture–*The Stocks*.
March 3, 1858

In 1858 the title 'Montgomeryshire Mercury' was in larger letters than 'Oswestry Advertiser'

Wynnstay Hall, which can be seen from the A483 near Ruabon, and is now a hotel, suffered a disastrous fire:

THE FIRE AT WYNNSTAY. DESTRUCTION OF WYNNSTAY MANSION, THE RESIDENCE OF SIR WATKIN W. WYNN, BART, MP.

We regret that we have this week to report one of the most calamitous fires that has ever occurred, within our recollection, in the Principality of North Wales. The extensive mansion at Wynnstay, the residence of Sir Watkin Williams Wynn, Bart, MP, was on the morning of Saturday last, almost entirely destroyed by fire.

The fire appears to have originated at about two o'clock on Saturday morning, but it was not discovered until after three, when it was found that there was a large quantity of smoke in the house, but up to that hour there does not appear to have been any blaze or flame. It is supposed to have commenced in a room under the library, although that is not certain, but as soon as the door of that room (from which a large quantity of smoke was issuing), was opened, a burst of flame broke out, and the whole of the adjoining rooms very rapidly ignited.

On the night of the fire, the occupants of the mansion, in addition to the usual establishment, were–Sir Watkin and Lady Wynn, the Earl and Countess Vane, and their two children, the Hon Col and Mrs Cotton, Captain Bulkeley, and Mr Hugh Williams.

The maid who was looking after Lord and Lady Vane's children noticed smoke in her room, and alerted everyone to the fire.

Everyone sleeping in the front of the hall, found that they had only just time to escape to their lives,–and Lady Wynn and the visitors could only throw around them one or two garments and so escape. Earl Vane on discovering the awful position they were in, exclaimed, "O God! where is my boy," and immediately ran to the bedroom where he was sleeping through fire and smoke, and brought him away in his arms.

We are glad to say, that the plate, and Lady Wynn's jewels, were all saved. At about five o'clock the fire was at its highest, and then the whole of the front of the hall was one fearful blaze, which raged with terrific violence, burning with an awful fury. The origin of the fire appears to be involved in mystery, though one is yet being able to suggest a cause for it. The house and premises being lighted with gas, no doubt added to the fury of the conflagration, but we have not yet ascertained that the fire was caused by the gas.

March 10, 1858

The house was totally destroyed, and 'not a wall that is left standing can be considered safe'. A proposal was put forward, which may surprise us; this correspondent certainly disapproved of it:

THE SYMPATHY OF SHILLINGS.

MR EDITOR,–Lady Wynn's jewels have all been saved during the recent disastrous fire. "No one," says the Vicar of Wrexham, "cares less for jewels than does Lady Wynn,"–*therefore*, the good people of Wrexham are getting up a "shilling subscription" for the purpose of presenting Lady Wynn with a casket of jewels!!!

Not a man amongst us, high or low, rich or poor, but thoroughly respects Sir Watkin; and all that have the honour to be, in the slightest degree, acquainted with his estimable Lady, love and venerate her,–but sympathy with them is not to be estimated by money, and such a contribution savours more of insult than respect!

I am, Mr Editor, yours &c, AN OSWESTRIAN
March 17, 1858

Before the abolition of the Borough Council in 2009 there were accusations about the duplication of local government; but such a complaint was not a new one:

Mr Editor.–If it be true that "too many cooks spoil the broth" in domestic life, it is no less so in public matters, and when a borough has too many governors, they generally manage to make a "pretty hash" of it. In Oswestry we have a corporation of Mayor, Aldermen, Town-councillors, &c, on the one hand, and a body of Street-commissioners on the other. These again are subdivided into a variety of smaller bodies, such as the watch-committee, the gas-committee, the committee for enquiring into the colour of the bellman's clothes, the market-committee, the scavengers' committee, the watch-the-interests-of-the-town Railway committee, and heaven knows how many more.
April 7, 1858

The Street Commissioners don't seem to have been improving matters anyway:

We have been requested to call attention to the state of Beatrice-street, but really we do not see that there is anything particularly the matter with Beatrice-street. It is in a very dirty condition; but are not all the other streets in Oswestry very dirty? It would be wonderful were it otherwise, when the authorities will not either allow the inhabitants to sweep them, or order their own scavengers to do so!
April 14, 1858

The house of industry, or workhouse, in Morda, was the place where the homeless went. There are several reports over the years similar to this one:

SERVED OUT!–A few weeks since two ragged rascals applied for a few nights lodging at the Morda workhouse. Finding their quarters rather comfortable they managed during the night to make such destruction of their unmentionables as to make it a matter of impossibility to any Master with pretensions to modesty to allow them to take their departure in the morning. One of them, brandishing in his hand the knife with which he had

rent his garments, vowed that the man who came near to him in order to take his measure for new clothing should be served the same as were the trousers. The Master, however, was equal to the emergency and taking up a pitchfork kept the fellow at bay while he sent for the tailor. The latter when he arrived proved himself an artist, and like the Master could "measure" the vagrants without tape and pencil. Obtaining two old rice bags he quickly split them up the middle and formed them into something like legs, then getting a tile brush he painted in bold characters up one leg and down the other–"Oswestry House of Industry". The Master, still keeping his hold of the pitchfork compelled his visitors to make a hasty toilet, and some of our townsmen, who happened to be abroad early on the morning of their exit, saw the crestfallen blackguards "making tracks" through the town, bearing on their persons an undoubtedly new order of "literary merit!"
April 21, 1858

The Bear Corner referred to the brothel area of Oswestry:

THE BEAR CORNER AGAIN! We had hoped that the abominable nuisance we sometime ago had so often to notice had been put an end to, but such we find is not the case; and yesterday three wretched looking creatures were brought before the Mayor, charged with robbing a farmer, residing near Whittington, of £20, on the previous evening. It appears that the man was drunk, and being met by one of the women, who is generally known by the name of "Miss Greasy Dick," was easily led into the house, and when there he had his purse taken from him.
May 5, 1858

There is some admiration and sympathy in this report for the poacher Tom Jones, a man who sounds very much like his namesake in the novel by Henry Fielding:

TOM JONES.–One of the most slippery gentlemen our police have had to deal with has been taken at last, and P.C. Titley has accomplished the capture. Tom Jones (against whom we never heard any charge brought, save that of poaching) was, on Friday morning last, about one o'clock, making his way up Bailey-street, when he scented a policeman, and being too cunning a fox to be easily caught, he at once hung down his head, and assumed the stagger of a citizen wandering home with unsteady gait, in a "state of beer." Titley accosted him, and not being satisfied with the mumbling reply, he lifted his head and identified him as a person "wanted" at Shrewsbury. Tom at once gave up shamming, and a fight commenced. Titley went down, and called out for assistance, hoping that his brother-policeman Turner was on padrole in the neighbourhood. Tom tried to stop Titley's cries, by placing his hand over his mouth to suppress them. His fingers slipped in, and Titley's teeth gave him a gentle reminder that they were not in the proper place. Titley then managed to rise, and they struggled together up the street, round the George corner, and to the Gaol

door. There a final struggle took place, and all was over with the poacher. There are now at least six convictions against Jones, and he must either pay some Twenty Pounds, or remain several months in prison. He was conveyed to Shrewsbury Gaol on Saturday.
May 12, 1858

There was a slight hope that the building of the Oswestry and Newtown railway was continuing, especially with all the local money put into it:

We may state with some degree of confidence that the works along the Oswestry and Newtown line of railway are progressing,–although the rate of progress is not such as to inspire the shareholders with a hope of speedy realisation of profits.
June 16, 1858

But the building of the new railway meant that, as if there wasn't already enough drunkenness in Oswestry, navvies were coming into town; although it doesn't seem to be altogether their fault if fights resulted:

SUNDAY IN OSWESTRY.–We are sorry to find that since the railway works have neared the town the inhabitants, have been annoyed more than once on Sundays, by the disgraceful conduct of some of the navvies. This is, perhaps, not altogether the fault of the railway labourers, for we have in our town a gang of idle and malicious vagabonds, whose chief business seems to consist in setting upon unwary countrymen, or any other workmen, whose business leads them into the borough for the purpose of getting a cheap fuddle by fair means or foul. On Sunday last, early in the morning, a fight took place near the Hayes, at which upwards of a hundred people attended.

One of the fighters was Dick Ty Coch, 'a well-known local pugilist' and someone who was often up before the magistrates for drinking and fighting. He, though, defends himself:

Dick, when brought before the magistrates, said that he could never leave the town in peace, the "town chaps" always set on him; and in this case his face corroborated his words, for he was terribly bruised. But Dick, being a well-known disturber of the peace, was fined £1 and costs.

Later on that same day, another fight took place at the bottom of the Butchers' Arms entry:

Shortly before two o'clock, Martin Flinn, John Flinn, William Tighe, and Dinnis McIvan, "navvies" went to the Butchers' Arms, where they sat drinking until three o'clock, and on leaving the house, Henry Middle, John Laurence and another Oswestry man came down Arthur-street, and Laurence pushing them said "Why don't you get out of the road?" John Flinn said "There's plenty of room" on which Laurence knocked him down! Laurence's party then called them Irish b——s, and on seeing his brother strike, Martin Flinn hit out at Laurence, and a general

row commenced, almost immediately George Farmer, William Jones (alias "Speed") and Thomas Evans rushed out of the Five Bells, and mixed in the fray. The younger Flinn swore that Farmer kicked him in the face when he was down, which statement Farmer denied, alleging that he was "too much a man to do it;"–for the time, we presume, forgetting, he was not "too much man" to let his wife and family starve, or "go on the parish" while he, an able-bodied mechanic was too idle to keep them! The elder Flinn swore that Evans kicked him when he was down, but George Russell was called as witness to prove that this was not the case, and stated that he saw Laurence do so several times. The only charge against Jones, was that he had hold of one of the Flinns when he was down, and was shaking him, at the same time shouting "They're only Irish, go into them!"
June 23, 1858

The Advertiser's Editor obviously had some extreme opinions about what to do with criminal children:

GARDEN ROBBERIES.–We are sorry to learn that garden robberies have been frequent of late, and would call the attention of the police to the fact. More than one amateur gardener has discovered the marks of little shoes around his gooseberry bushes; if the owners of these could be caught, a public whipping at the Bailey Pump might be of service.
June 30, 1858

There was much speculation nationally about a comet that was seen in the sky, and whether it was going to hit the Earth:

"COMET (very) EXTRAORDINARY."–A correspondent of the *Manchester Examiner* on Saturday writes as follows:–"About eight o'clock on Wednesday morning last, a comet was seen going from east to south-west, at Llanyblodwel, near Oswestry. It appeared to the naked eye to be about the same size as the sun, with a tail about three yards long. It was visible twice,

In February 1858 Richard Myddleton-Bddulph of Chirk Castle was 21

for some seconds each time, the sky during that period being of a rich purple." We wish "Our Correspondent" had given his name, and stated what he had taken for supper on the previous evening, and we should have been the better able to understand this wonderful phenomenon; as it means we can only fancy he must have stumbled over that old pamphlet, "Will the approaching comet strike the Earth?" For strange enough, as far as we can hear, this wonderful comet has only been seen in the columns of the *Manchester Examiner*.
August 25, 1858

Oswald Road did not exist before the main railway station was built. It was called, at first, New Road. The 'old station' mentioned here was the GWR station:

THE RAILWAY STATION.–We are happy to inform our friends, that the site of the new railway station is at last definitely fixed upon. It will be erected within a few hundred yards of the old station, and just at the back of the late Mr James Vaughan's premises in Beatrice-street. There will be an approach made from Leg-street, opposite the Cross Keys. We understand that the alterations will be commenced almost immediately.
October 13, 1858

It seems the Castle Bank was not going to be open to everyone:

THE CASTLE BANK.–We are glad to find that the parties who are interested in making the Castle Bank an attractive promenade, and an ornament to the town, have taken some steps in order to put a stop to trespassing. The parents of those children who are in the habit of running over the Castle Hill as they would over a Turnpike Road, will do well to prevent continuance of the practice, and all trespassers had better be cautious.
October 20, 1858

As Christmas approached, some levity crept into the reporting:

CRINOLINE AGAIN.–*A Fact*.–A lady in Oswestry the other evening, in proceeding to take a chair at the head of her table, insensibly pushed it away from her, with the expansive crinoline she wore, and found herself,–to the no small amazement of her guests,–on the floor!
December 8, 1858

This old character had lived through much:

DEATH OF AN OLD SOLDIER.–In our obituary this week we recall the death of John Edwards, one of the "oldest inhabitants" of Oswestry. As a lad he "served the bricklayers" during the close of the last century, and about the commencement of the present, being fired with the glories of war, he listed in the 86th Regiment, and went out to India. His campaigning did not last long, for in 1803, at the taking of Bhurtpoor, he had a leg shot off, and was soon afterwards discharged on a shilling a day pension. For upwards of 50 years he has lived to enjoy this in Oswestry; and in many a

party of old soldiers as he fought marvellous battles over again! He was well known in the town as the husband of "Peggy Julius," and the father of "Jack Spanker," a brace of worthies who died before the sire.
December 22, 1858

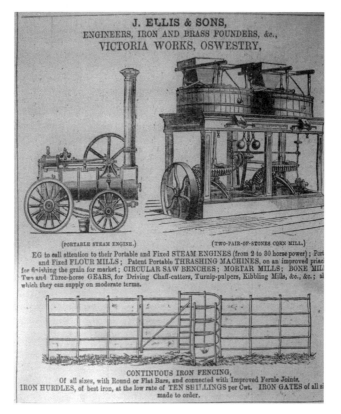

J. ELLIS & SONS,
ENGINEERS, IRON AND BRASS FOUNDERS, &c.,
VICTORIA WORKS, OSWESTRY,

(PORTABLE STEAM ENGINE.)   (TWO-PAIR-OF-STONES CORN MILL.)

EG to call attention to their Portable and Fixed STEAM ENGINES (from 2 to 30 horse power); Port and Fixed FLOUR MILLS; Patent Portable THRASHING MACHINES, on an improved princ for finishing the grain for market; CIRCULAR SAW BENCHES; MORTAR MILLS; BONE MIL Two and Three-horse GEARS, for Driving Chaff-cutters, Turnip-pulpers, Kibbling Mills, &c., &c.; al which they can supply on moderate terms.

CONTINUOUS IRON FENCING,
Of all sizes, with Round or Flat Bars, and connected with Improved Ferule Joints.
IRON HURDLES, of best iron, at the low rate of TEN SHILLINGS per Cwt. IRON GATES of all si made to order.

STEAM THRASHING MACHINE.–On Wednesday last, August fair day, a novel spectacle was witnessed on the Bailey Head, in the shape of one of the steam thrashing machines lately exhibited at the Chester Show. The machine in question was manufactured by Messrs Ellis, of Oswestry, and was greatly admired at Chester for its compactness and utility.
August 11, 1858

It seems that shops were usually open over most of the Christmas period, except for Sundays:

HOLIDAYS.–Notwithstanding the refusal on the part of some of the trades-men to close on Monday last, several adhered to their bond, and "shut shop," although the holiday was not recognized as a general movement. On Saturday next the usual New Year's holiday will be observed. We are not aware that any of the tradesmen refuse this date to their assistants, and it is to be hoped that the "customers" will make their purchases on Friday. If the public would only remember the day, there would be no need of any of the young men remaining in the closed shops, in order to attend to the wants of the thoughtless.
December 29, 1858

In Oswestry there was another case concerning the famous and troublesome Middle brothers. It seems it was a familiar practice to toss a coin to see who would pay for a round of drinks:

Robert Evans said–I was in Oswestry on Monday night last, in company with four fellow-servants. We came from Halton after supper to buy some clothes; it was nine o'clock before we got to Oswestry, and when we had made our purchases we went to the Horse Shoe, where we had four or five pints of ale amongst us. Henry Middle was there and a blacksmith of the name of Edwards. After we had the drink there were some tossing between myself and Henry Middle. I won a quart and he paid straight and we had it in. He wanted me to toss again, but I would not. The blacksmith and Henry Middle left the house directly afterwards, and I followed them in a minute or so. As I got to the door someone pushed me, I found it was George Middle: he missed, pushing me down, and Henry Middle tripped me up, and fell over me. They all then kicked me when I was down, and when I got up they tried to throw me again. I had an ash plant [*a stick*]in my hand and struck at them with it. George Middle got it from me and struck me with it several times. They all three then set on me once and I shouted "murder." The Middles then ran away but I held the blacksmith by the hair of the head until Mr Jones the policeman came up and took him into custody. P.C. Turner and Jones went with me down to the Middles' house by the New Church. They came out and challenge the police and any of us to fight.

But the defence maintained that it wasn't the fault of the Middle brothers at all, but the countrymen's. George Morris, a shoemaker, gave his version of the affair:

I saw the rout commence in the street; they were all standing round the door of the Horse Shoe and Morris's entry. Henry Middle was on the causeway and Evans by the gutter. Someone, I don't know who, shoved against Henry Middle and he fell against Robert Evans. I don't believe it was done designedly. They were all the worst for liquor. When Henry Middle and Evans were down, the countryman came up and laid on Henry with an ash plant. Another of their party came up and kicked Henry, on which Edwards the blacksmith said "I can't stand to see that" and ran in and began to lay about him.

The magistrates chose to believe the countrymen's' story, and George Middle was fined £3 and costs. A similar charge was preferred against Henry Middle, and the same fine inflicted. The Advertiser made this comment:

We have had too often occasion to notice the shameful way in which the bullies of town attack the countrymen, and the ingenious construction put on this affair, by the witness for the defence, does not make this case any less flagrant than former ones. The countrymen were doubtless very much to blame to stay in a public house until such an hour, and we are sorry to say that three of them were lax, who one would think ought not to be

allowed to come to the town at all at so late an hour; but while they were in the town they ought not to be the subject of such shameful abuse.
January 26, 1859

At last something was being done about the Castle Hill:

It gives us great pleasure to be able to state that there is every prospect of the Old Castle Hill yet becoming a credit to the town. When it was first enclosed and planted, a period of some three or four months of drought followed, in consequence of which, half of the trees and shrubs died, and, the place not being systematically looked after, the remaining half were so trodden down by the juvenile Arabs who infest the borough, that they never had a fair chance of arriving at maturity. Just now, we are glad to say, Mr Dicker, surgeon, whose taste as a florist is very well known, has kindly volunteered his services as custodian of the hill, and already does it wear quite a new appearance. Something like 200 firs have been planted, chiefly on the bleak side; some rustic seats have been placed here and there, and flower seeds, we understand, will be sewn as soon as the owners of poultry in the neighbourhood can be persuaded to find some other promenade for their cochins!
February 9, 1859

Thomas Savin (*see biography on page 156*), the draper of Oswestry, had moved into many ventures, including hop merchant and owning a coal pit at Coed-y-go, near Morda. Now he started a very different enterprise. He was introduced to David Davies of Llandinam, and the two of them began to build railways, starting with the Vale of Clwyd in Denbighshire. The building of the Oswestry and Newtown railway had come to a halt when the contractors went bust, so it was a chance for Savin to do something nearer his home town:

Rumour has been afloat in Oswestry during the past week to the effect that the spirited contractors of the Vale of Clwyd and Newtown and Llanidloes railways (Messrs Davies and Savin) have made a liberal offer to the board of the Oswestry and Newtown railway to complete the line forthwith.
The works between Oswestry and Welshpool are in a tolerably forward state. We understand that a small, compact station has been erected at Llanymynech, and it is confidently stated that the Oswestry station is about to be commenced at once; but our readers in the immediate district will be sorry to hear that the contract at which it is taken is so low that, at best, we can only reasonably expect a third class, roadside station! An engine is now

The first cover for 1859

daily expected and will be placed on the line below the Salop-road Bridge. This will look like business!
February 16, 1859

An interesting verdict at this inquest — the verdict now would perhaps be 'natural causes':

It appeared that on Tuesday last Mrs Franklin, a widow, had not been seen about all day, and on her daughter trying her door she found it was fast. Mrs

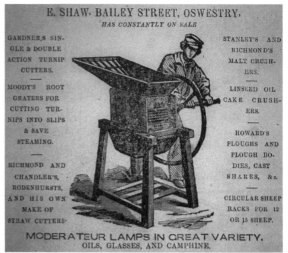

Franklin's son, on bursting the door, found the old lady dead on her chair. A verdict of "died by the visitation of God" was returned.
February 23, 1859

This is a gently satiric comment on the lack of progress of the Oswestry and Newtown Railway:

For the benefit of those who have not heard the news, we must announce that an engine, called "The Shark," has just been placed on the rails of this line, at the Oswestry terminus. We are requested to say that the name of "The Shark" is purely accidental, and has no reference to any party now connected or who has at any time been connected, with the company's affairs.

We are happy to say that the works are progressing favourably. Four men and a boy have been working more than "half-time" between Oswestry and Pool Quay during the past month, and there is every prospect of the line being completed in the present, or at any rate, the next century.
March 30, 1859

At the General Election of 1859 there appears not to have been a Liberal candidate, much to the annoyance of the Advertiser's publishers, who were staunch Liberals:

"Long life and prosperity to Mr J. R. Ormsby Gore" stares us prominently in the face as we perambulate the street of Oswestry, and in this we add a hearty "Amen." Had a Liberal candidate come forward we would have done all we could to ensure his return. But as a Liberal did not come forward, we deemed it the next best thing to try and persuade liberals not to vote at all!
May 4, 1859

These were dubious qualities for the keeper of the lock up:

> At a meeting of the Watch Committee, held on Saturday last, P.C. Williams, the gaol keeper, was charged with insubordination to the superintendent, and also with being frequently drunk, and consequently disqualified to attend to the duties of his office. The charges were proved, and Williams discharged from the force.
> *May 4, 1859*

Davies and Savin were still trying to get the contract for the Oswestry and Newtown Railway, and the Advertiser was on their side – only partly because the editor was well acquainted with Thomas Savin, of course:

> The question will naturally be asked, "How can Davies and Savin offer better terms than other contractors?" It is enough for us to know that they do, and that they are men who well know what they are about. But, whatever their reasons may be, we are glad to be assured that they can and will finish our line.
> *May 18, 1859*

This kind of accident unfortunately still happens:

> MELANCHOLY ACCIDENT.–On Wednesday evening, as some children were going along the canal side to some fields adjoining, to gather cowslips, one of the party, a little boy about four years old, son of Mr John Morris, sawyer, of this town, became sulky and stayed behind, and all the others returning they discovered the hat of the little fellow floating on the top of the water, and not finding him, they immediately gave an alarm. Search was made in the canal, and not long after the body was taken out of the water just as the police arrived with drags.
> *May 18, 1859*

George Owen was someone who became very prominent in the town, as Mayor and Chairman of the Cambrian Railways. He brought Davies and Savin together.

> APPOINTMENT OF SURVEYOR.–We have much pleasure in announcing that our townsman, Mr George Owen, C. E. was appointed, on Saturday last, successor to the late Mr Penson, as surveyor of the Oswestry District of roads.
> *June 29, 1859*

This letter draws attention to a danger that is probably rarer now – driving over donkeys:

> SIR,–I wish to draw the attention of those who have the care of the roads around Oswestry, to the greater number of animals, especially asses, there are constantly straying about the said roads, by day and by night, to the annoyance, and to the endangering the necks of travellers. A gentleman told me the other day that he once had his vehicle upset at night by driving over one of the nuisances I have alluded to, and several pedestrians I have heard complaining of these impediments being allowed to remain

on the public roads. These animals are chiefly kept by the idle and the lowest part of the population, and are becoming a common nuisance. Hedges are damaged, fields and gardens are often invaded, horses frightened, and lives (as I have before stated) endangered! Hoping that this matter will be taken up, and attended to at once,

I remain, Sir, your obedient servant, CLEAR THE ROADS.

July 6, 1859

An important step for Oswestry was having the offices of the Oswestry and Newtown Railway in the town:

The offices of this railway company have, at last, been removed to Oswestry, where the interests of the shareholders have long since pointed out that they ought to be stationed. The rooms selected are part of the late Cross Keys, which are admirably adapted for that purpose.

July 27, 1859

Davies and Savin were proving themselves excellent contractors by making good progress in a short time:

A rumour is current that the Oswestry and Newtown Railway is to be opened as far as Llanymynech "in a month."

August 3, 1859

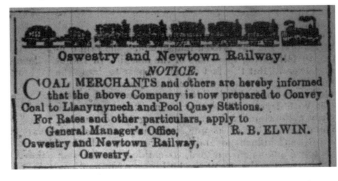

Oswestry and Newtown Railway.
NOTICE.

COAL MERCHANTS and others are hereby informed that the above Company is now prepared to Convey Coal to Llanymynech and Pool Quay Stations.
For Rates and other particulars, apply to
General Manager's Office,   R. B. ELWIN.
Oswestry and Newtown Railway,
Oswestry.

And, sure enough, a month later:

The works between Buttington and Welshpool were commenced on Monday, by Messrs Davies and Savin, and will be prosecuted with vigour. We are now informed on good authority, that the directors do entertain the idea of opening the line for traffic between Oswestry at Llanymynech before the remainder of the works are completed.

August 17, 1859

This letter had a sly and surely unfair dig at postmen:

MR EDITOR.–It is currently reported in Oswestry that our letter carriers are to be provided with red coats as well as new bags. This is a "step in the right direction," but if we are to have a good stride, let the Postmaster general offer a premium for a "regulation seven league boot," so constructed as to pinch the toes of the postmen, when they stand still for more than

the necessary time at the door. And as every garment now-a-days is registered under some high-sounding name, call the one I recommend the "Antigossipingmoveon Propeller."
Yours &c, A Fast Man.
August 24, 1859

The Advertiser was again campaigning for shop assistants, and their long hours:

The question of how many hours constitute a day's work is becoming just now more than ever exciting. The "building trade" are of opinion that ten hours work is too much, and think they are not unreasonable in asking that nine hours constitute a working day. What do we say of the shop assistant? Shopmen have never less than 12 hours, and on two days in the week, 14 and even in some cases sixteen hours toil!
August 31, 1859

There were still complaints about the state of the roads:

Sir.–Our good old town is notorious for the accommodation afforded to pedestrians by having neatly kept foot paths upon the side of each row leading from the town. But while those side parts are so well kept in good order, other parts are so neglected that they are almost impassable, and almost speak in language as plain as if a notice was stuck up with the words, "No Road here."
Your obedient servant, A Walker
September 28, 1859

There's a certain stubbornness shown by John Owen here, which didn't do him much good:

A wife deserter.–On Monday last, John Owen, lately an auctioneer in Oswestry, was charged with deserting his wife and family, whereby they had become chargeable to the parish. Mrs Owen gave her evidence, after which Owen cross examined her as to her means of maintenance. His object was to prove that he had not run away, but had left with her knowledge and at her request, and that since he had left he had not earned enough to keep himself in the bare necessaries of life. Owen was sentenced to 21 days' imprisonment, which he said, "I'd sooner stand on my head double that time than support her." Mr Venables then recalled his sentence, and gave him two months. On leaving the court, Mrs Owen asked her husband to speak to the children before he went, but he turned his back on them, and was marched off to the lock-up.
September 28, 1859

Only a few months after Davies and Savin had taken over the building of the Oswestry and Newtown Railway:

We believe the 20th of October is the day now fixed upon the opening of the Oswestry and Newtown Railway to Pool Quay (which is within 4 miles

of Welshpool); but, as there is yet a good deal to be done before it will be ready to passenger traffic, it may be the end of the month before the opening takes place.
October 5, 1859

A complaint that seems universal, about people, especially young people, hanging about on the pavements:

Sir,– In Oswestry, anyone would suppose that the causeways were made for lounging places, and the dirty street for promenading; for, from my window I often see ladies compelled to go off the foot paths, because the enamoured youths, who are, generally in clusters, talking to highly-flattered housemaids at the end of entries, cannot think of giving them room to pass; or because of the gangs of hulking vagabonds, who think they have a constitutional right to the corners, and who would not budge an inch, were the Mayor and Corporation marching past in state procession. Yours obediently, An Invalid.
October 12, 1859

There were still complaints about the street lights:

Sir,–Will you allow me, through the medium of your columns, to enquire who regulates the time of lighting and extinguishing the lamps in our town? As to the time of lighting, I have no cause for complaint, but in reference to the time of extinguishing the lights, there is just course. I had occasion to get up this morning about five o'clock, and as soon as I put my head out of doors, I found the streets in total darkness. I can hear vehicles passing down the street, but it was impossible to see them until they were within a very few yards.
I am, Sir, your obedient servant, Luminous
October 19, 1859

Already, after just ten years of having a railway in Oswestry, there were articles looking back on the days of slow transport; but this gives an interesting idea of the itinerary and speed of a stagecoach:

Before the invention of railways it was extraordinary in what ways and means our forefathers had of getting over the ground. "The Original London and Shrewsbury Fly" was to do the journey in thirty hours! It was evidently a very desirable conveyance in its day, for it went "on steel springs, with chairs on the top, by way of Coventry." It started from the Queen's Head, at four o'clock in the morning, "breakfasts at the Red Lion, Shiffnal, set out from thence at 7 o'clock to the New Swan, Wolverhampton, where it arrives at 9 o'clock, and will arrive at the George Inn, in Digbeth, Birmingham, at 12 o'clock, where it will dine, and set out for London at three o'clock, and will arrive at the Blossoms Inn, Lawrence-lane, Cheapside, London, the next day;" but where the passengers are to sleep, unless it is on the "chairs" over the "steel springs," we are not told! Fancy, in this

Welshpool School.

PATRON :—THE EARL OF POWIS.

FOUNDER :—THE VEN. ARCHDEACON CLIVE

VISITOR :—THE BISHOP OF ST. ASAPH.

PRINCIPAL :—Mr T. B. BROWN.

MODERN LANGUAGES :—MONSIEUR TERRIEN.

THE EASTER TERM will begin on MONDAY March 30th, 1868.

Pupils are prepared for the Law, Preliminary, Oxford Middle Class, and Civil Service Competitive Examinations.

Oldford, Welshpool, March 24th, 1868.

age, staying about as long in Birmingham to dinner as would complete the journey to London by rail! The fare for the journey, exclusive of the multitude of ostlers, boots, waiters, and other hangers on of coaching places–all of whom would expect fees–was £1 16s., inside places, "outsides as usual," whatever that may have been.
October 19, 1859

Davies and Savin proved that they could build railways with the speed they completed the Oswestry and Newtown Railway:

The first locomotive engine (which is called the "Wynnstay") arrived a few days ago, and on Monday a trial trip took place when Mr Savin, Mr Piercy [the engineer], and several other gentlemen, went ten miles up the line. The trial was in every respect satisfactory. Messrs Davies and Savin have two other engines ready–viz., the "Glansevern" and the "Montgomery"– one of which arrived yesterday.
October 26, 1859

Even in 1859 people were saying, 'We expect something better from the youth of our day':

A NEW "DEAD SET."–Some five and twenty years ago, a party of young men were in the habit nightly of prowling about the borough, taking down loose signboards and wrenching off old established knockers. Those were "good old times" when mechanic's institutions, reading rooms and cheap newspapers were unknown. We expect something better from the youth of our day, and suggest to the Corporation the advisability of getting a new stocks made forthwith to be in readiness should a recurrence of the scene enacted in Arthur-street a few nights ago, take place.
November 9, 1859

There was more unusual weather at Christmas:

THUNDERSTORM AT CHRISTMAS.–On Friday last, Oswestry was visited by a storm, the like of which is unremembered by "the oldest inhabitant." About three in the afternoon the sky became clouded, and in a few minutes the atmosphere became exceedingly dark, and a high wind arose, followed by heavy rain. Almost immediately a vivid and prolonged flash of lightning lit up the heavens, followed closely by a loud peal of thunder. The storm lasted nearly half an hour, during which time the thunder and lightning continued.
January 4, 1860

Once more, there was a proposal to enlarge the Oswestry Advertiser.

This paper has now stood the test of Twelve Years, and may be considered fully established as a First-class Medium of communication in all matters of Local Interest to the Border Counties. The proprietor has determined considerably to enlarge the paper, without any advance of price.
January 18, 1860

This refers to Oswald Road, then called New Road:

THE NEW ROAD TO THE STATION.–We are glad to say that several men are now engaged in clearing the rubbish away, and otherwise preparing the road that is to lead to the new station. We hope that no obstructions, other than this *materiel*, will prevent the work being shortly completed.
February 1, 1860

The reporter writing about this case tried very hard to capture the accent in this fight between two Irishmen:

THE IRISH YARD.–Robert Delaney said, "Patrick Hardiman came into my house on the seventh of Jaynewury an' trottled me wid his fingures against de wall." Hardiman, however, gave a very different version of the story, he said he had been in Delaney's house about an hour and a half, they had some rum, which he was dividing with some neighbours. Delaney's step-son had bought the rum, and had asked him to divide it. Delaney came in mad drunk, and all he did to him was to catch him by his shoulders to prevent him doing mischief. Case dismissed.
February 1, 1860

Superintendent Sykes seemed to have made an impressive start in cleaning up crime in Oswestry. But then came this case at the magistrate's court, and it proved disastrous for Sykes's career:

FOX VERSUS SYKES, FOR ASSAULT.

John Fox.–I am an auctioneer, and the secretary of the Savings bank. On Saturday night last I left the Unicorn Inn about ten o'clock, to go home.

I turned aside at the end of the Temperance House, for a necessary purpose. Just as I did so, Mr Sykes came up and collared me. I asked him what he wanted, but he did not answer. I then said, "If you want me, my name is Mr Fox." He still collared me, and I caught him by the whiskers and we both fell; he was bottom. Mr Lowther, Mr Jones, and some others came up. I called for a second-class constable, but no one came, so I said, "I'll turn policeman myself." I then charged Sykes with being drunk, and said that I would take him to gaol. Those who came up asked me what we were doing, and the crowd soon collected, some of whom commenced snowballing us most unmercifully (Laughter). The assault I complain of is that he collared and cuffed me.

There seemed to have been some past history between Fox and Sykes, but Fox maintained:

I was not drunk. I had had two glasses of ale at the Grapes, one at the George, and one at the Unicorn that evening. Sykes and I have had some differences before. I have had an altercation with him about the gas at the Powis Hall. I did on one night shout at his window, "Put out the gas, you fellow!"

Fox had several witnesses to support his case against Sykes, including one John Jones, who said:

I was told that there was a row on the Bailey Head, and when I got there found Sykes holding Fox by the neck. Fox said, "Loose me, what have I done?" Sykes did not reply.

Cross examined–I never had any ill will towards Sykes. I was sorry for him, he was very drunk, I wanted to get him home. Some of those who had gathered about were snowballing him. I then went to Fox's house. I do not think he was perfectly sober.

James Jutson, butcher–I was at my standing on Saturday night last. Sykes came into the market soon after nine o'clock. He said to me, "Well, have you been cursing and blasting anybody today?" He stunk of

ELECTRICITY IS LIFE

PULVERMACHER'S PATENT

GALVANIC CHAIN BANDS

enable every sufferer to benefit, at a small expense, by the wonderful curative properties of Galvanism in the most severe cases of Rheumatism, Neuralgia, Paralysis, Epilepsy, Sciatica, Head and Tooth Ache, Deafness, Nervous Debility, and all Functional Disorders. According to the seat of the disease the Chain Bands are adapted to be worn on any part of the body affected, with the greatest ease and comfort. Their prolonged, efficacious, and perceptible action is entirely in harmony with the Nervo-Electric vital power of our organs, promoting digestion, circulation, &c., and restoring in a most natural way a healthy state of the Nervous System. Numerous striking documents, reporting their extraordinary efficacy, are compiled in a pamphlet "PULVERMACHER'S IMPROVED MEDICO-GALVANIC SYSTEM OF SELF-APPLICA-TION," (post free for 3 stamps), by J. L. PULVERMACHER & Co., 73, Oxford Street, London, (adjoining Princess' Theatre). Chain Bands, 5s., 10s., 15s., and upwards, according to their electric power.

AGENTS– Mr W. Griffith, surgeon, Oswestry; Mr Witney, chemist, Shewsbury; Mr T. Kemble Williams, chemist, The Cross, Welshpool.

drink like a pig (Laughter). I thought he wanted to insult me, and I turned away from him, or I should have knocked him down.

Other witnesses were called to prove that Sykes was drunk. Mr King, of the George Inn, stated that Sykes was staggering, and that his wife was trying to get him home. King said that Sykes called them all a set of scoundrels, and said all the town were scoundrels. There was only one witness for the defence, Superintendent Sykes himself. He said that Fox had been talking to a woman, something that Fox denied, and no other witness observed:

William Sykes–I was going up Bailey-street from the market on Saturday night. I noticed a man and woman close together by Mr Davies, machine-maker's door. I slackened my pace, and the woman stepped from the man, and said, "I give this man in charge." I asked her what she charged the man with. She said, "He has insulted me, but I am ashamed to say how." I kept my eye on the man, who was stooping, with his hands before his face. I went and took hold of him, and said, "Turn to the light, my man, and let's see what you are like." He turned round, got my stick, and knocked me down. I then discovered that it was Mr Fox. He went towards the Red Lion. I followed him, and he struck at me again, and we had a wrestle for the stick. I said, "You have assaulted me, and I will take you in custody for it." While we were wrestling some people came up. They all said I was drunk. I scarcely said a word. The snow and splash came every minute. My wife came and said, "Loose him, and come home." I did loose him then, for I saw there was no chance. When I lost my grasp, Fox held his hands up and said, "Now I'm free; I'll take the superintendent up." Fox caught hold of my arm, and said, "Come along." My intention was to lock Fox up when I got into the gaol.

Sykes was asked how much he had had to drink, and he replied, 'I don't know. I don't keep an account of what I drink,' to which there was laughter.:

The court was then cleared, for the magistrates to consult together, and when the public were readmitted, the Mayor said–We think that the evidence is in favour of Sykes and we acquit him of the charge of drunkenness. We fine Mr Fox 5s. for the assault.–The decision seemed to cause considerable astonishment.

It wasn't surprising that the verdict caused astonishment, when so many witnesses supported Fox and none Sykes. Letters came in to the Advertiser:

Dear Sir,–This is not the first, second, nor third time that rumours have gone abroad in Oswestry that Mr Sykes was not a man of perfect sobriety; and it has been said that witnesses were ready to prove the charges rumoured against him. The town council very properly took no notice of these vague charges. Now, however, the case is very different, and although he is acquitted by the magistrates, the council have to bear in mind that 12 witnesses appeared, who distinctly swore that he was drunk!

I am, dear Sir, yours, &c, A tradesman.

An editorial also appeared:

> There is a strong feeling in the town condemnatory of the Superintendent of Police, although he was acquitted by the magistrates. We are sure our worthy magistrates will agree with us that there was much in Sykes's conduct which demands an investigation by the Town Council.
> *February 8, 1860*

Sure enough, at the end of the month a meeting of the Watch Committee, which was in charge of the police, was called:

> Having duly considered the whole of the circumstances connected with the conduct of Mr Sykes, the superintendent of police, we come to the conclusion that Mr Sykes, in going to several public houses in succession throughout the evening, and drinking with different parties there, was guilty of gross misconduct, and that such conduct was unbecoming a police officer. We, the committee, therefore give it as opinion, that we do not consider Mr Sykes to be a fit person to be at the Head of the Police of this Borough, and we leave the final determination thereon to the council.

The council, though, gave him one last chance, after a reprimand:

> Sykes then addressed the Council with reference to his conduct in the last ten years, in terms not very derogatory of himself. He expressed his thanks to the council for dealing so leniently with him, and said he could not justify his conduct on the occasion referred to.
> *February 29, 1860*

This case shows the dangers and troubles of being a young servant with a violent master:

> Richard Thomas, a boy of about 12 years of age, summoned Mr Wylde, his master, on a charge of having violently assaulted him. Richard Thomas said–Mr Wylde sent me to Weston Mills with a load of wheat, and afterwards to Maesbury Marsh for some coal. I came back at nine o'clock and went into the house to light a candle. Mr Wylde was in the kitchen, and scolded

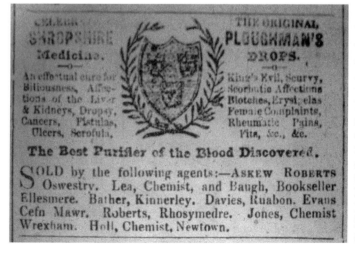

me for having been so long, and then knocked me down with his open hand and kicked me. He then pulled me back again, and kicked me again, hurting me severely on the side. The next day I went home and saw the doctor, and did not recover for a week.

Plaintiff's mother, on being called, said that her son came home and said his master had been beating him. He took off his clothing, and showed her his side, which was all bruised and raw. Her husband spoke to Mrs Wylde about it, and she said he was drunk and like a madman that night. He asked Mr Wylde in the morning what he had been abusing his boy for, and Mr Wylde said he deserved abusing.
February 29, 1860

In April, the New Road (later Oswald Road) was opened, with the open sewers, the mud pits, removed:

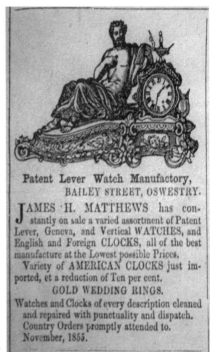

Patent Lever Watch Manufactory,
BAILEY STREET, OSWESTRY.

JAMES H. MATTHEWS has constantly on sale a varied assortment of Patent Lever, Geneva, and Vertical WATCHES, and English and Foreign CLOCKS, all of the best manufacture at the Lowest possible Prices,

Variety of AMERICAN CLOCKS just imported, et a reduction of Ten per cent.

GOLD WEDDING RINGS.

Watches and Clocks of every description cleaned and repaired with punctuality and dispatch, Country Orders promptly attended to.
November, 1855.

Within half an hour of the time that the last load of gravel was laid on the New Road, heading from the Cross Keys to the Railway Station, the omnibuses had taken possession; and on Monday last, "all the (Oswestry) world and its wife" promenaded the whole of the afternoon. Messrs Davies and Savin, the spirited contractors, deserved the thanks of every man, woman, and child in Oswestry, for the work they have so thoroughly performed. They have removed the greatest nuisance the town ever possessed, and, in its place, have made the greatest improvement the town has seen for many years. The older mud pits were to Oswestry what the Thames is to London; but with this drawback, they were only a nuisance, and of no earthly use what ever.
April 18, 1860

William Ormsby Gore was MP for North Shropshire from 1835 to 1857. He was born William Gore, and when he married Mary Jane Ormsby, daughter and heiress of Owen Ormsby, he assumed the additional surname of Ormsby. He was the great-great-great-great-grandfather of the present Lord Harlech. Porkington, presumably an Anglicization, was the name then used for Brogyntyn:

THE LATE WILLIAM ORMSBY GORE, ESQ.

It is our sorrowful duty this week to record the death of Mr William Ormsby Gore, who expired at his residence at Porkington, on Friday morning last, in his 82nd year. He leaves a widow and two sons, the elder of whom is MP for North Shropshire, the younger for the county of Leitrim.

May 9, 1860

There was an excited announcement about the railway between Oswestry to Welshpool:

On Saturday last it was rumoured that one of the greatest wonders of the world–a Railway Locomotive–would, before the people were two days older, actually run on iron rails into the town of Welshpool!

May 23, 1860

Once again youths were misbehaving:

THE HORSEMARKET.–Attention was called to the fact that several of the windows in the Powis Hall were broken. This was stated to be done by boys who were playing at ball in the Horse Market. It was thought the attention of the police should be directed to the matter, and that offenders should be punished.

May 30, 1860

A serious railway accident happened near Oswestry station, on the GWR line. Amazingly no one was killed even though two carriages fell down the embankment:

An engine, pushing a lot of empty cattle trucks up the line towards Oswestry Station, came to a standstill about 80 yards below the railway bridge over the Whittington Road, and the passenger train from Gobowen junction being due, the guard in charge of the trucks went down the line with a danger flag, but too late to prevent a collision; for, just at the same moment the train came up, and the sharp curve at that particular spot prevented the driver from seeing his danger until he was close upon the trucks.

The driver of the passenger train stuck to his post, and did all in his power to decrease the speed, but such was the force of the blow, that both engines were considerably injured and the tender run into was so damaged that some of the heaviest bolts were twisted like wire. The passenger engine was partially thrown off the line. The two carriages immediately following were thrown down a fifteen-feet embankment, with such force that one was completely swept off its wheels, and the other turned upside down. Being Oswestry fair day there were considerably more than the usual number of passagengers, and it is marvellous that some fatality did not occur; but it providentially happened that in the two carriages overturned there were comparatively few passengers.

June 13, 1860

With no mains water supply, only wells, a water cart was bought by the Street Commission:

THE WATER CART.–A correspondent writes to ask, "Why, in the name of fortune, the water cart ordered by the Commissioners some months back and received into Oswestry some weeks ago, is never used?" He presumes that the Commissioners are "waiting until we have more wet weather," as such a course would be "quite consistent for a body who have a regulation authorising the gas lights to be put out on certain nights into, however dark if the moon happens to be at the full in the almanacks."

July 11, 1860

In this case a man left his son with his parents so the son could look after them; and the grandfather sued his son for the boy's upkeep:

The father, a joiner, in Oswestry, sued his son for 22s. which he stated was due for his son's little boy. Defendant denied the debt and said that his little boy was there to assist the old people, and his mother was quite surprised at the case being brought forward. He had done a good deal for his parents, and had never let them want for food. His Honour said it was humiliating to see such cases in a Christian Country; South Sea Islanders would never act so.

August 1, 1860

At last, thanks to Davies and Savin the Oswestry and Newtown Railway was opened to Welshpool:

This gives a foretaste of the future, when not only two isolated towns in one county should be united, but when every principal town in the county should be brought within a few hours'

ride from the metropolis of the kingdom, and within a short distance from the great metropolis of manufactories, and from the leading seaport towns of England.
August 15, 1860

Almost immediately, however, there were complaints:

DEAR SIR.–I trust some arrangements will be immediately adopted to avoid the absurdity of changing carriages at Oswestry for the sake of the three miles run to Gobowen–this is outrageous.
Respectfully yours, T.G.
August 22, 1860

It's clear why a new gaol was needed in the town:

Near the Horse Shoe Inn P.C.Jones found Edwards with nothing on save his trousers, making a great row, and challenging some men to fight. Jones first tried to persuade him to dress and go away peaceably, but he refused to do this, so was taken to the lock-up. Superintendent Sykes deposed that on Tuesday morning P.C.Turner sent for him to the gaol as Edwards was pulling the place down. He went and handcuffed him, and placed him in another cell, where he became still more violent. The magistrates went to the gaol to look at the damage done, and found one cell floor covered with bricks and mortar, the prisoner having torn the brickwork asunder, and almost succeeded in effecting an escape into the yard. The second cell was almost in as ruinous a condition, although the man was handcuffed.
September 19, 1860

Now that the railway was almost finished all the way from Oswestry to Llanidloes, there were more ambitions – a line to Whitchurch through Ellesmere:

On Monday last, a most important public meeting was held at the Bridge-water hotel, at Ellesmere, in furtherance of a scheme to connecting the towns of Oswestry, Ellesmere, and Whitchurch, by means of railway communication, and thus placing them on the great through route, from Manchester to Milford. The want of a railway has been long felt by the people of Ellesmere.
October 3, 1860

At first this seems simply a report about a typical drunken Saturday night in Oswestry, of perhaps any time in the last few hundred years:

We hear from several quarters that every Saturday night, or perhaps it would be nearer the mark to say every Sunday morning, the peaceful repose of the townsfolk in different parts of the borough is disturbed by the shouting, fighting, and other disorderly conduct of a gang of black-guards who set law and order at defiance. Many complaints have been made to the police, and on Saturday night last, the streets being more than usually thronged with unruly spirits, the police made a capture of seven, three of whom were of the gentler sex, but not by any means favourable specimens!

However, the report turns into another attack on Superintendent Sykes, this time for locking up the wrong people, especially three women, Ann Edwards, Eliza James, and Ann Golligher:

Ann Edwards, a respectable looking young woman, who has of late taken to evil ways, was charged with being drunk and fighting with her brother in Bailey-street, at half past 11 o'clock. In defence, Edwards said that she was not fighting, and that the blows her brother gave her were only for her good. Owen Edwards, the brother in question, was charged with a breach of the peace. He had come from the Duke of Wellington, and seeing his sister in the street, commenced beating her. In defence, Edwards said he was vexed to see his sister going with bad men. Mr Jones said he did not wonder that he should feel pain at his sister's conduct but he should take a more gentle way of trying to reclaim her.

Eliza James, charged with being disorderly. Superintendent Sykes said she was one of a new importation of prostitutes lately arrived in the town, and that she was coming out of the Duke of Wellington with a lot of men, very noisy.

The third case involved a famous character of the town, Dick Ty-coch (sometimes spelt Ty Coch):

Ann Golligher was charged with making a disturbance in the streets. In defence she said that she was only shouting after Dick Ty-coch, the father of her five illegitimate children, who did not support them, although she had sworn them upon him. The magistrates told her she ought to get a warrant, and not make a noise in the streets. She said she was unable to procure money for a bit of meat, much less for a warrant. Discharged.

There were others who were making a noise, but in each case they were being sorted out before the police arrived:

Richard Williams was charged with making a disturbance in Brook-street, and his brother, Isaac Williams, with aiding and abetting in his escape. P.C. Roberts said that Isaac Williams had held his arm when his brother got away. Williams said that his brother's wife came to him and asked him if he would go and persuade him to go home, as he was not sober. He went to do so as the police came up, and laid his hand on Roberts's arm, and said he would see his brother home. Mr Sykes ordered that they should both be locked up. Mr Jones thought Isaac Williams was doing a very kind action and that the police ought to be glad of the help of such a man. Case dismissed, the magistrates say that they were very sorry that Isaac should have been in custody.

Thomas Williams, charged with "howling in a lane leading to Penylan." (This is really the only way in which we can put the charge.) Mr Sykes proved the howling, and gave an illustration in court; and supplemented that Williams was drunk. Eight witnesses said that Williams was not drunk.

Each case was dismissed. The Advertiser suggested that the police, and Superintendent Sykes in particular, were being too heavy-handed, often arresting the wrong people. It then asked if a county police force ought to replace the town one:

That great disturbances did take place on Saturday night there is no question, and that the police did exercise considerable agility is equally apparent,–and they are to be commended for it,–but we fancy if we lost "our power" by letting in the county force, we should get a superior officer who united "discretion" with other qualifications.

October 17, 1860

The Great Western proposed a new line, from Rednal to Oswestry, mainly because it wanted to build the new line from Oswestry to Whitchurch; if a line from Rednal had been built, Oswestry would still have a railway, as it would be on the Chester to Shrewsbury line:

A scheme said to be in contemplation by the Great Western company for placing Oswestry on the main line, will be affected by the making of a new portion of railway from Oswestry to Rednal; Gobowen, as a junction, will be shut up, and Whittington, we presume altogether abandoned, as a passenger station.

October 31, 1860

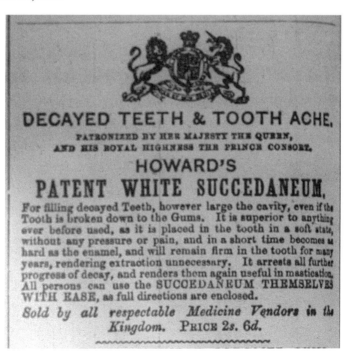

The Oswestry and Newtown Railway had only been open a few months when it had its first accident, though this guard seems very unlucky:

It appeared that William Southcott, a guard of a luggage train, was assisting to shunt the trucks. The driver received a signal to advance, as he did so the firemen noticed someone on the rails, and whistled loudly; this not being attended to, the brake was put on, and the engine reversed; at the same moment, Southgate stepped off the line, and leaned against a carriage which had been placed so close to the crossing, the corner of it was over the line the engine was on, just at the spot where the deceased leaned. The unfortunate man was immediately torn in pieces.
January 2, 1861

This is another case of the mistreatment of a servant:

DISGRACEFUL ASSAULT.–Mary Jones was a servant at Sweeney, and went to a dressmaker in Morda, on a commission for her mistress; she returned at about eight o'clock, and finding the house locked up, called to Richard Tunley to open the door; he came downstairs, and when complainant had come in, he threw a vessel full of "lant" or putrid urine into her face, and that without the slightest provocation on part of the girl.–The magistrates considered this a most disgraceful case, and fined the defendant £3 and expenses, or one months' imprisonment in default.
January 2, 1861

Some gentle sarcasm was used to point out the poor timekeeping of the town's clocks:

A MARVELLOUS FEAT.–A correspondent writes:–"Allow me to call your attention to a wonderful feat which I performed on Friday last.–I started from the Bailey-head just as the Bailey clock struck ten, and walked slowly (as I imagined) down towards the old Church. I stopped for a minute or so to speak to a friend on the way; but, nevertheless, incredible to relate, I arrived at the church at *two minutes to ten!* So that, unless the clocks were wrong, which of course is out of the question, I actually walked a distance of about two hundred yards in two minutes less than in no time! To prove that there is no jugglery in the matter, I will go through the performance again on Wednesday next, at the same hour. No charge will be made to spectators, but a box will be handed round afterwards. I must, however, stipulate that the clocks shall not be meddled with in the meantime."
January 23, 1861

This man misused the market to make some money, with the Advertiser asking again for its favourite means of punishment:

P.C.Jones said that George Roden, a wandering dealer of all work, who lives upon his wits, was in the habit of buying pigs from those who brought

them to the fair, and if he failed in getting a customer from whom he could realise a profit, he refused to pay the owners, and the fair being over, they had to take the pigs home again. If the poor people said anything to him, he would curse them until they were afraid to say a word. Fined 5s. and costs. We may remark that in this case the fellow (who richly deserved a heavier punishment than a mere money fine) told the bench he was unable to pay. And the Borough not being in possession of a stocks, he was allowed to go at large, under a promise that he would pay the next time he came to Oswestry! It is surely time that a stocks should be procured.
February 13, 1861

This case seems rather unfair on William Pearson:

CHILD DESERTION.–William Pearson, a navvy, was charged with neglecting his children. He denied the charge, and said he had never left them; they shared all he had, and when he was out of work, of course he could not feed them. He was now in work, and would be very glad to contribute to their support, if they should be left in the house of industry. His wife had left him nine months ago, so we had no one to look after them, and if he stayed at home himself, he would lose the means of supporting them. The case was adjourned.
February 20, 1861

The Borough police force was amalgamated in February with the county force, which meant that the town could get rid of Superintendent Sykes at last. He was given a gratuity of £35. His last case in Oswestry he lost, which often happened with him. It was a case where he thought he was being bribed, but it may have been that he simply didn't understand what was going on:

Superintendent Sykes said:–John Weston came to my house at 12 o'clock on Wednesday night and said he wanted me to go and apprehend a man who had insulted him. I went with him to the Queen's Head to see for the man. When I got there he asked me to take a glass of sherry, this I refused. He then said that this was not the house he was insulted in. We then went up towards the Wynnstay Arms. On our way up Church-street, he said Mr Laxton, of Shrewsbury, had been robbed of £50, and said if I would go with him to some house where we could have a room to ourselves, he would give me some clue to the perpetrators of the robbery. As we were coming down Leg-street, I said come in the Cross Keys, then we can have a private room. When we got in he asked me again to have something to drink, I said I would not, and he then said he would not tell me unless I would take something.

At this point Sykes said Weston dropped some money, which Sykes suspected was an attempt to bribe him.

As we were coming up Beatrice-street, he said I hear your force are going to join the rural force, and that you will lose your situation, therefore you must need money. He then put two pounds in my hand, and said, I have got a friend in gaol, and as you are going to leave in a short time it would not be much for you to put him right. I then took him into custody as a suspicious character.

Weston's version seems to show Sykes's incompetence:

Last night I was insulted in the town, and I went to Mr Sykes to obtain assistance, as we were coming from Sykes's house, he told me he was going to leave this situation, and had a large family to support. I then (being half drunk at the time), gave him £2, a thing which I could ill afford to do. The case was then dismissed.
March 13, 1861

It seems here that William Evans was leading on Anne Lewis:

A LADIES MAN.– Anne Lewis sued one William Evans, tailor, for the sum of 11s, money lent, and shop goods. Defendant denied his liability on the ground that the lady was anxious to have him altogether, and accordingly took him out for walks, and in their rambles turned into sundry public houses where she stood treat, he drinking whisky and she preferring rum. One day, said the defendant, "she said to me and says, 'let's get married' says she. I says, 'never, says I, you have had a child by another man and I cannot entertain the idea,' says I." Here His Honour interposed with the enquiry as to how he met the claim for borrowed money? In reply the defendant contended that he did not have any money but the lady was suing for the treats she had stood. She had offered money for him to go and get a licence. His Honour again interposed and asked why they did not get the banns put up? "Oh" replied the defendant, "I suppose she preferred it quick!" His Honour told defendant his conduct was disgraceful.
May 8, 1861

Perhaps here, for once, the Advertiser wasn't quite correct in its prediction:

THE OLYMPIC GAMES.–The committee of gentlemen who have been so zealous to establish games in districts "all around the Wrekin" similar to those held in ancient times in the city of Olympia, seek for their object to promote "the moral, physical, and intellectual improvement of the people, by the encouragement of outdoor recreation, and by the annual distribution of prizes to skill in military and athletic exercises, and proficiency in literary and fine art attainments." All this looks extremely well on paper, but we have strong doubts of the ultimate success of the experiment. We fear the whole business will turn out in the long run to be a mistake.
May 22, 1861

At last there was a railway all the way from Oswestry to Llanidloes:

OSWESTRY AND NEWTOWN RAILWAY.–We are glad to say that at length the Oswestry and Newtown railway has passed through all its preliminary stages, and that it is now perfectly ready for passenger traffic from beginning to end. The line may be regularly opened for traffic, when we believe the trains will run through from Oswestry to Llanidloes.

June 5, 1861

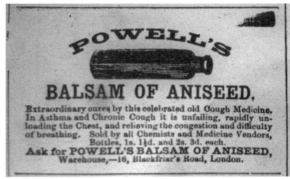

POWELL'S

BALSAM OF ANISEED.

Extraordinary cures by this celebrated old Cough Medicine. In Asthma and Chronic Cough it is unfailing, rapidly unloading the Chest, and relieving the congestion and difficulty of breathing. Sold by all Chemists and Medicine Vendors, Bottles, 1s. 1½d. and 2s. 3d. each.
Ask for POWELL'S BALSAM OF ANISEED, Warehouse,—16, Blackfriar's Road, London.

There had been a long battle at the Houses of Parliament, between the GWR and the independent Oswestry, Ellesmere and Whitchurch Railway, as to which company would build the railway through Ellesmere. The town generally favoured the independent company, believing the GWR to have treated the town badly, especially when one of its barristers famously called it "the wretched little town of Oswestry". The winner was announced, with no doubt as to their popularity:

> The news of the success of the independent line was received here with an unbounded satisfaction. The town was the scene of continued emotion after one o'clock on the following morning, bellringing and cannon firing being the order of the evening.
>
> *June 26, 1861*

The success of the Oswestry, Ellesmere and Whitchurch Railway was due largely to the efforts of Thomas Savin (now no longer in partnership with David Davies), but there was obviously some snobbery amongst his critics, as he was still known as the "small haberdasher". However, he had many friends in high places:

> When Sir John Kynaston said before a committee of the House of Lords "I believe the Oswestry people are entirely indebted to Mr Savin for the Oswestry and Newtown railway" the worthy baronet uttered no more than the simple truth. And when he further stated "I can say nothing but good of him" the cheer that would have been given but for Mr Dennison's warning "hush" would have testified how far Sir John's testimony found a response in the breast of the numerous representatives of this district, who were present in the committee room. The manly declaration of the baronet, who lives in the house where his family has lived for seven centuries, was a severe approve for those who would taunt Mr Savin with having been a "small haberdasher".
>
> *July 3, 1861*

Savin wasted no time before beginning the new railway:

> Three days after the celebrations for the opening of the completed Oswestry and Newtown railway, the Oswestry, Ellesmere, and Whitchurch

railway had a celebration of the ceremony of cutting the first sod, at Ellesmere.
August 10, 1861

There was a brief and hopeful announcement for the Advertiser:

On and after August 7, the OSWESTRY ADVERTISER will be published TWICE A
WEEK, every WEDNESDAY and SATURDAY without any additional charge.
July 31, 1861

But only a month later another one:

After a month's experience we find that although sales have been increased
by the change, there is a very general feeling amongst our subscribers in
favour of the old plan of once a week, and in deference to these wishes
we propose to return to the issue of one double paper every Wednesday.
The Advertiser will consequently be published on Wednesdays only at
Twopence, and will contain 48 columns, being about Eight columns more
material than formerly appeared in the weekly issue.
August 31, 1861

This shows a great expectation of the Post Office, that we probably wouldn't have
now:

SIR,–On Friday last, I wrote to a gentleman residing near Chester appoint-
ing a meeting on the following morning at Shrewsbury, and of course I
was there prepared to meet him, but to my surprise he was not there at
the appointed time, so my journey to Salop was to no purpose, and on
Monday I received a note informing me that my letter had not got to hand
until Sunday morning.
Yesterday evening, I happened to travel to Shrewsbury by the train leaving here at 9 p.m. which train carries Oswestry letters. When we got to
Salop Station I found that the North Western mail train had gone, and
upon enquiry one of the officials there inform me that it was not an unusual occurrence, as it missed three times last week, and the mailbags were
then left in Shrewsbury all night. This accounted for the disappointment
I experienced on Saturday. Hoping something may be done to prevent so
much inconvenience,
I am, Sir, yours truly, A TRADESMAN.
September 4, 1861

Turnpike gates took money from travellers, to pay for the upkeep of the roads. But
there could be problems collecting the toll. There is a great deal of uncertainty as to
where exactly was Carneddau Road; it seems to have been on the Welsh-facing side
of town. Bertie Wynn was the man who donated the fountain at the Cross:

DRUNK AND EVADING TOLL.–John Colley and William Evans were severally
charged with being drunk, and the latter with using abusive language. It
appeared from the evidence of Mrs Preston, who keeps the Turnpike gate,

on the Carneddau Road, and Mr Bertie Wynn, who was passing with some ladies at the time, that the accused were driving at a furious rate up the road, and did not stop to pay when the toll was demanded. Mr Wynn, fearing that Mrs Preston would be run over, interfered, when Evans got out of the cart, called him abusive names, and lifted his whip to strike him. The men both seemed to be drunk, as they could not sit straight in the car, and one tendered his hat in payment of toll.

Both defendants denied they were drunk. Evans said he had not tasted a drop of ale or strong drink for 18 years, but:

He admitted speaking sharply to Mr Wynn, "which not knowing he was a gentleman, and which he did not act as such, interfering where he had no business." They both declared that they had no wish to evade the toll, and Evans said it was paid before Mr Wynn interfered. The magistrates thought drunkenness was proved in both cases, and fined Colley 5s and Evans 20s, and costs.

October 2, 1861

Another drunkenness case involved someone pretending to be a doctor:

A "MEDICAL MAN" IN TROUBLE.–Yesterday afternoon, a man named William Mason, a quack doctor, was charged with being drunk. From the evidence of Sergeant Gough, who brought the charge, it seems that on Monday evening, Mason impudently went to a house in Willow-street, where a young woman, who was in lodgings with her mother, was ill,–and said he had been sent there to give her some medicine. He then mixed something in a bottle, and said it was 2s 9d, which sum he demanded. The young woman and her mother refused to pay it, and then Mason, who was drunk, began to create a disturbance, which led to Gough being called in, when he took him into custody. The prisoner admitted the charge of drunkenness, and he was fined 5s and 4s costs. Having only 1s 2 1/2d to pay it, he, (vigorously assisted by his wife), begged for time to get it,–and said if he should be allowed a day or two, he would come and "pay it like a gentleman." He was allowed a week to get the money.

October 30, 1861

Railways were very dangerous then; as soon as the Oswestry and Newtown Railway opened, there was an accident on it, near Montgomery:

> A sad accident occurred on this line on Saturday morning, by which William Bakker, engine driver, and Marmaduke Harrington Kerr, fireman, met with instant death.

The goods train came off the rails, as it was going too fast, though at only about 30 miles an hour – new lines had to be driven on carefully. The likely cause was the behaviour of the railwaymen when the train stopped at Abermule for twenty minutes. The guard told the inquest:

> We went into the public house at Abermule. William Bakker, who was driving, and Kerr, who was Stoker, and Shaw, who was a guard of the train, were all on the train. We all went into the public house. We were in the public house about five minutes. We had two glasses of rum and milk each.
> *November 13, 1861*

After having small stations since the GWR reached Oswestry, the impressive (and still standing) Cambrian Railway Station was being built:

> The managers of the Oswestry and Newtown Railway are to be congratulated on the fine open weather they have had during the past month for the furtherance of the work of building now going on at the various stations. Substantial warehouses are nearly finished at two or three of the stations; and to us, most important of all, the Oswestry Station works are speedily rising above the ground. Hope deferred has made a public heart very sick, and to see a commodious and well-arranged station in the course of rapid erection in Oswestry rejoiceth it exceedingly. Right glad are we to report progress concerning such enterprising men as Mr Savin, and those who are in conjunction with him. We understand that all the woodwork of the Oswestry station has been in preparation for some months, so, if the weather remains fine, there is no reason why the building should not be ready at an early date.
> *December 4, 1861*

In December Prince Albert died at Windsor Castle, from an attack of gastric fever:

> As in every other town in the kingdom, signs of the sorrow felt for this mournful event have been everywhere to be seen in Oswestry during the whole of the past week. Every tradesman we believe without exception, left up at least one shutter on his shop windows, and on Monday (the day of the funeral) in compliance with a request from the Mayor, the whole of the shops were closed entirely, and business in a great measure suspended. On Sunday the pulpits in the various places of worship in the town, were hung with black cloth and in the Old Church the communion table, the mayor's pew, and other parts were also similarly draped.
> *December 24, 1861*

The Oswestry Street Commission was abolished, so from now on the streets would be the responsibility of the Town Council:

> Oswestry has seen the last of her commissioners, and the loss will only, we trust, be felt as a gain by the borough. About a dozen members met on Monday and quietly and deliberately signed their own death warrant. Well, it was a useless body, and had only power to make half-measures, and powerless to carry even these out. Now, however, if our town council choose to do so, they will have full powers over nuisances inside and out of sight, private drains as well as public sewers, the market halls, and the streets; and it is their fault, and theirs only, if Oswestry does not become a model borough for business, health, and cleanliness.
>
> *January 1, 1862*

Dick Ty Coch appears again:

> AN INCORRIGIBLE.–Richard Jones, *alias* Ty Coch, who has been repeatedly before the magistrates for the non-maintenance of his illegitimate children, by Ann Gollicker, was again brought up on Monday. The woman is now in the House of Industry, and with her five children, are chargeable to the parish. Jones said he would pay so much a week, but this promise had been so often made and broken, that the magistrate sent him to gaol for two months. It appears that when P.C.Lloyd went to apprehend him, under the warrant at the suit of Ann Gollicker, he found him in a field working. Jones took up a heavy bill hook, and threatened to cut open Lloyd's head with it. Lloyd was obliged to leave him, and seek assistance. When he returned with P.S.Gough and another officer, Jones again flourished his hook, and they were obliged to use considerable force. Jones denied that he had attempted to strike the officer. He was working with the hook.
>
> *January 8, 1862*

The Cambrian Railway Station was now almost a storey high. It was completed later in the year:

> We are glad to see that the station will really be ornamental as well as useful, and will be a credit to our town, which sadly lacks respectable looking public buildings. This station adds another to the many benefits conferred on the borough by our enterprising townsman, Mr Savin.
>
> *January 15, 1862*

The fountain that was recently put back at the Cross was built in 1862:

> We understand that Mr Bertie Wynn, of Llanforda, has signified his intention of presenting to the town a handsome fountain, to be placed in the Cross, on the site of the present ugly lamppost, and uglier pump. The design, we believe, is a very elegant one, and is surmounted by a cross,

The three faces of the Cross fountain

which will be appropriate in a place that only retains the name of what was once doubtless an ornament in that position.
February 26, 1862

Night soil is human excrement collected at night for use as a fertilizer, and the law seems to have been strict as to when it could be collected:

An offence against a street act.–Sergeant Gough found the defendant and a boy, between ten and eleven o'clock in the forenoon, wheeling the night soil from his yard into the yard belonging to Mr Evans, builder, where a man was loading it in a cart. Told him that it ought to have been emptied between the hours of 11 p.m. and 5 a.m.
April 2, 1862

At the inquest for this sexton it was said he was known to say, 'repeatedly, that he would lay violent hands upon himself'. There does seem to have been some macabre behaviour in the crowds that 'thronged':

Shocking suicide.–On Sunday last, this town was thrown into a state of considerable excitement, owing to the report being spread about of the death of Charles Jones, the sexton of the old church, by his own hand. He was discovered at a quarter past ten o'clock, on Sunday morning last, by his wife (who had not seen him since noon the previous day), lying full-length on the floor of the shop in a pool of blood, with his head nearly severed from his body. Crowds thronged round the door of the shop where the deed was done, all day on Sunday, to catch a glimpse of the man whose name had been known as a household word, and whose death had created such excitement and horror amongst the townspeople.
April 9, 1862

Oswestry Races were revived this year, and on the Old Racecourse, even though books about Oswestry Races state that the last races were held there in 1848:

For many years the sporting inhabitants of Oswestry and vicinity have been debarred from following their favourite pastime at home, and have been dependent on neighbouring towns for the enjoyment of the old English sport of horseracing. This year, however, an attempt has been made to resuscitate the time-honoured anniversary on Cern-y bwch, which, considering the short time that has elapsed since the event was decided upon, has met with considerable success.
April 9, 1862

A Ragged School was an attempt to give education to the poor:

A meeting was held at the Wynnstay Arms hotel, upon Friday last, to consider the advisability of forming a Ragged School in this town.
June 4, 1862

This case reads like an episode of a 19th century soap opera:

DOINGS IN HIGH LIFE.–Mr Richard Price, chimney sweeper, and smoke jack cleaner, was summoned by Miss Louise Harriet Hotchkiss for an assault. The complainant said–I met defendant's daughter and asked her quietly for some things of mine she had had to pledge twelve months ago. While I was talking to her, the defendant came up and called me a very bad name. He then gave me a blow in the face, the result of which was a black eye. He afterwards struck me several times.
Defendant said–I went to look after my daughter on the day in question, and I was quite surprised to see her talking to that woman, the complainant. I then told her to come away from "that brute." The present case is only got up because the complainant is jealous of me. I had got married on the morning of the assault, and that was the way she wanted to annoy me. She struck me first. It is altogether jealousy on her part, because if she had been a prudent woman I should have made her my wife; but she is not prudent, and I know she would swear the leg off an iron pot (laughter).
June 4, 1862

Whenever a tramp behaved in this way, the heading was the same:

THE HEIGHT OF IMPUDENCE.–John Brown, a tramp, was charged with stealing from a boy, aged nine, his dinner. It appears that the little fellow was going along the Moreton-lane, Parish of Oswestry, with his dinner in a basket, when he was met by Brown, who asked him what he had got? The boy replied "dinner," whereupon the rascal took the basket from him. The one cried lustily, and the other eat heartily. The scamp was afterwards apprehended, and was committed to take his trial at the next petty sessions.
July 23, 1862

In August the final decision was made to allow the Oswestry, Ellesmere and Whitchurch Railway to be built. This was mainly thanks to the efforts of Thomas Savin, and when he arrived back at Oswestry this was how he was greeted:

SEE THE CONQUERING HERO COMES!
What shall we say to the reception of our townsman Mr Savin on Wednesday evening? Mr Savin has so recently been among us,–one of ourselves–a shopkeeper; that some of our townsfolk have been slow to believe that there could have been anything but the merest accident in his rising from the position of a haberdasher measuring out the tapes and retailing bobbins, to that of a contractor, laying down miles of railway and entering into engagements involving hundreds of thousands of pounds. But when we have found, day after day, week after week, that our trade has been

increasing, our town has been enlarging, and our commercial prosperity, generally, has far exceeded that of any former time, it has begun to dawn upon us that Mr Savin is something more than the creature of accident. That he has a head to plan as well as the energy to carry out, those magnificent schemes, which will eventually place Oswestry, second to no town of its size in the kingdom. That when we are on the MAIN LINE FROM MILFORD HAVEN TO MANCHESTER, and are enjoying the increased prosperity such a position will give us, we shall be able to say with pride and satisfaction, that we owe our position to the tact, talent and energy of a fellow townsman.

This must have been the peak of Thomas Savin's career, to come home to such a reception:

At the railway station crowds of people were in waiting from eight o'clock, for although no announcement had been made of the fact, it seemed to be ready generally known that Mr Savin would arrive from London soon after nine. The train pulled up at the station, and in the saloon carriage were, Mr Savin, Mr Hilditch, Mr G. Owen, and other gentlemen, officials and supporters of the Oswestry, Ellesmere and Whitchurch railway. The platform was lined with tradesmen and other inhabitants of the town; and the hero of the hour was evidently, for the moment, considerably non-plussed, and looked very much as if he wished to beat a speedy retreat. He was, however, at once apprehended, and was compelled to give way to the force of arms which hurried him into the carriage in waiting.

As may be supposed, a procession by torchlight, amidst a dense crowd of people, in the narrow streets of our little town, is no very fast affair, and it was some time before the top of the new road was reached. At that point the Oswestry Rifle Corps band struck up the air, the name of which heads this report.

August 6, 1862

from The Story of the Cambrian

There was still opposition to Savin, with snobbery the probable cause:

> We are informed, but we are loath to believe it, that some parties in this neighbourhood have threatened to withdraw their subscriptions to the Oswestry Rifle Corps, under the belief that the band of the corps played "See the Conquering Hero comes" before Mr Savin, in his triumphal procession through the streets of Oswestry, on Wednesday evening week.
> *August 13, 1862*

This is another soap opera case, and difficult to see if it's merely a misunderstanding, or something more serious:

> THE COST OF A KISS.–Elizabeth Jane Brumman summoned Thomas Davis, both of Oswestry, for an assault, alleged to have been committed on her, by kissing her.
> Mrs Brumman, on being sworn, said–I being in want of a house, went to Mr Davies, to enquire the rent of the new houses that are in the course of construction by the Rope-walk. He invited me to see his garden, and pointed out to me where he was going to build in the garden. After walking a little in the garden, he asked me to sit down, which I refused to do. He then pulled me down, and said, "I must kiss you." I got up from there, and I walked away, but he brought me back and kissed me. I went to the gate of the garden and tried to go out; at last he opened the gate and let me out. I was walking away, and when between two walls that leads to his garden, he called me, and squeezed me in a very improper way.
> Cross examined–We did chat rather freely. I was not laughing and talking. I only laughed at the absurdity of the thing–he wanting a kiss when I said to him no (Laughter).
> Mr Jones–Were you not quoting poetry to one another. Quoting either Byron or Moore?
> Plaintiff.–No, he repeated poetry to me, and I only wish I could remember it.
> Mr Jones.–Was it very nice?
> Plaintiff.–No, it was not.
> Mr Jones.–Then why do you wish to remember it?
> Plaintiff.–Because, then I would tell it to you. I know what was the purport of it, but I told him I was true to my husband. I did not ask for a rose. He gave me a rose, and I said it was very pretty. He gave me the rose after he had kissed me, and at parting by the garden gate, he asked me to say nothing about the matter. I don't think I should have said anything if it had stopped there, but I tell you he followed me, and between the two walls heading to his workshops and garden, he improperly laid hold of me. I was not afraid of being seen with him because I thought I was walking with a respectable man.
> The bench having decided that the assault was committed, fined the defendant 10s, and 10s 6d costs.
> *September 3, 1862*

There were occasionally much more violent and dramatic cases. This was one of the most serious, even if when it reached court it sometimes descended into farce. It deserves telling at some length, as it eventually went to the County Court:

DARING HIGHWAY ROBBERY, WITH VIOLENCE.

On Monday night, the quiet town of Oswestry was alarmed by the report that a murderous attack been made on some parties close to the borough. It appears that Mr Oswald Davies, with Miss Thomas and Miss Matheson, had gone for a walk along the high road to Shrewsbury, shortly before nine o'clock. The night was fine and moonlight. Just as they passed through the turnpike gate they saw four men sitting on the roadside, one of whom asked them to relieve him. Mr Davies gave the man a copper, on which he grumbled, and demanded sixpence, which Mr Davies refused, and, with the ladies, went on down the road. When they had gone a couple of hundred yards they turned back and almost immediately met the four men. One of them demanded Mr Davies's money, and another seized Miss Thomas by the throat. Mr Davies resisted, and the other two fell on him and overpowered him, beating him over the head with a heavy stick, until he was rendered partially insensible. Miss Thomas was thrown to the ground, but Miss Matheson managed to escape, and ran towards the town.

Miss Matheson found help, but by then the men had run away, with Mr Davies's watch and some money.

We are sorry to add that Mr Davies was very roughly handled, his clothes were literally torn to pieces, and his head very much cut and bruised by the brutal attack.

Four men were soon arrested for the crime:

Benjamin Davies, alias "Ben the Ostler," and John Delaney, who were suspected of being the principal actors in this brutal outrage; and Robert Green and John Hughes, alias "Bunter." They are now lodged in the Oswestry lock-up. We believe they will be brought before the magistrates today, and then be remanded to enable the police to get up the case.

At the magistrate's court Oswald Davies told the story of the attack, and it's interesting that the perpetrator liked to use the language of the traditional highwayman:

The man took hold of me by the collar, and said "stand and deliver." He had a stick in his hand, which he held over his shoulder, and he then said "your money or your life." I said "don't be foolish," and endeavoured to pass on. He then threw me down, and I received three blows on the head with a stick. The other men were by, and two of them assisted him, but I could not see very well, as I was down. I told them they should have my money, and was putting my hand in my pocket to get it, when I found it was gone. It only amounted to a few coppers.

The main question was who had done it. Benjamin Davies, alias Ben the Ostler, was allowed to ask questions of the witnesses, as was the custom in the court then. Oswald Davies answered him:

I know you by the expression of your face and general appearance. I did not know you by any particular marks on your face. I noticed the colour of your hair.

Prisoner–Had I no cap on that night? How could you see my hair?

Witness–I believe you had a cap on. I could see part of your hair. I could not describe your cap.

Prisoner (touching his side locks)–Was this the same sort of hair I had that night?

Witness–Yes, I believe so.

Prisoner–Then you will swear anything, if you will swear that! When did you see me last before this?

Witness–I don't remember any particular place where I have seen you. I did not say you were a native of the town. I know you belonged to the town, because I had seen you before. I cannot say where or when.

Prisoner–That's a singular thing to me, gentlemen. It's no use asking you any questions.

By prisoner Hughes–I won't swear that I saw you.

Hughes–What's the use of me axing him questions then (laughter).

By Green–I am not sure that I saw you there.

By Delaney–I have not sworn to seeing you.

The next witness was Miss Thomas, who said:

I found myself on the ground with a man's hands on my shoulders, which he slipped to my throat, and he turned my head with my face towards the hedge. My head was turned from Mr Davies. I thought that was done to prevent my seeing them. I was conscious from the scuffle that they had taken Mr Davies to the other side of the road. I stopped there a little time, when the man pressed my throat more, because, as I believe, he thought I was going to scream. There was no attempt to rob me. One of the men said, "We won't hurt you, lady."

Miss Matheson corroborated the evidence of her friends.

I can recognize one of the men in the dock. The man on the left, with a light-coloured cap on (Davies).

Prisoner Davies.–Did you ever see me before today?

Witness.–I believe I saw you that night. I am as certain as I can be of anything.

Prisoner.–Was I looking you in the face when you saw me?

Witness.–No, you were not looking me in the face.

When in December the case came before the Shropshire Assizes Ben the Ostler again put up a strong defence, even if the judge didn't appreciate it:

Oswald Davies said to the prisoner Davies–Your face was quite familiar to me. I should call your hair red.

Davies–My hair proves itself, my lord, that it's not red. (Laughter).

Oswald Davies–I could see the stick behind you, although you were in front.

Davies–Then I suppose you have eyes behind you. (Laughter).

His Lordship–Ask questions. We are not here to listen to your attempts at wit.

Oswald Davies–The moon was clouded, but I could see.

Davies–Why don't you speak up. My guilty conscience does not prevent my speaking up. (Loud laughter).

His Lordship–There is such thing as a scared conscience, prisoner.

Davies–Then why did he laugh at me.

His Lordship–I did not see him laughing.

Davies (impudently)–Perhaps you wasn't looking.

Davies then cross examined Miss Thomas:

Davies–Do you know the nature of an oath, my wench? (Laughter).

His Lordship–Prisoner, I will not allow you to speak this way to a lady. Ask your questions properly.

Davies–She's so dull, my lord (Signs of disapprobation).

After a few more questions, Davies made a sudden attempt to get off his shoe, but was detected by P.S.Gough, and that officer called to the turnkey, who, after a struggle, wrested the shoe from him.

Prisoner Davies–That was stopped by you, Gough, you b—y b—r, I wish I had you here.

After all his questions of the witnesses, attempting to disprove he was the man who had committed the crime, Davies finally admitted:

I own I am guilty, but I am sorry for these poor lads. Young Davies says I asked for sixpence; I did not. I was in a state of abject poverty, and when he gave me the penny, I said to the other men, "That makes sixpence towards our lodging." This made Young Davies think I asked him for sixpence. I was in my own town, but could not go for relief, because, being a notorious poacher, and having struck a policeman in the Five Bells when I was tossicated, I could not go to the police.

The jury brought in a verdict of guilty against Davies, but didn't think there was sufficient evidence to convict the others, and so gave them the benefit of the doubt.:

His Lordship then addressed Davies, and said that he had been previously convicted of felony at Oswestry, and had been sentenced to four years' penal servitude at Maidstone Assizes, but he had not profited by the punishments he had received. His Lordship then sentenced him to 12 years' penal servitude.

Davies–You had better give me twenty, my lord, and then I shall go to the colonies. I would rather have twenty, for your lordship does not know what tyrants we meet with at home; but woe be to any tyrant that tries it on me!

Ben the Ostler certainly seems to have been something of a desperate character, even if a fairly intelligent one. This is the rather comic postscript after the case:

During the hearing of this case, the prisoner Davies behaved in so violent a manner, that three or four turnkeys and policemen were placed around the dock to guard him. At one period of the hearing, he was observed to take a piece of paper from his pocket, and to attempt to put something in his mouth, and one of the offices, fearing that it might be poison, caught him by the wrist, which Davies became frantic, struggled violently, and swore most fearfully. The court was at once thrown into confusion, and the word "poison" having been loudly exclaimed by one of the parties in the dark, his Lordship called out "Send for a *surgeon* instantly." The Chief Constable of the county, hearing this imperfectly, and having an unbounded faith in his own retainers, shouted, "Let a *sergeant* go into the dock!" and confusion was made the worse confounded by the arrival of an officer of that rank, accompanied by a couple of constables, who only served to choke up the already overcrowded space in the dock. In spite of this accession to the discord, however, comparative calm was restored, and the trial proceeded.

September 10 & December 10, 1862

A great event happened in Oswestry, that was going to put Oswestry on the map, because soon half of the great Manchester to Milford Railway was complete. It needed a great procession to celebrate the event:

CEREMONY OF CUTTING THE FIRST SOD OF THE OSWESTRY, ELLESMERE, AND WHITCHURCH RAILWAY, AT OSWESTRY, ON THURSDAY, THE FOURTH OF SEPTEMBER, 1862.

Punctually at 12 o'clock the procession left the Bailey Head, and proceeded down Bailey-street, through the Cross, up Church-street, down Lower Brook-street to the Dispensary, thence along Roft-street to the new church, up Salop Road to the Cross Keys, through Leg-street to the new road, passing the new station, by the terminus of the Great Western company into Beatrice-street, thence to the Shelf-bank field, where the ceremony was to take place. With respect to the number who appeared in the possession it was said to amount to upwards of 3000 persons, and so far as respectability is concerned, it was one that, in its appearance, did credit not only to Oswestry, but would have been respectable in a town of much greater importance.

September 10, 1862

PIANOFORTES.

EDWARD EYELEY, Organist, and EDWARD JONES, Upholsterer, beg to inform the inhabitants of Oswestry and neighbourhood, that they have made arrangements for keeping a stock of PIANOFORTES by Collard and Collard, Broadwood, Hopkinson, and other makers.

A selection of Instruments by the above makers may now be seen at E. J.'s Show Rooms, Cross Street, Oswestry.

This year the family Hughes, all with the nickname 'Bunter', kept appearing. One of them, John Hughes, had been arrested but acquitted in 1862's highway robbery on the Shrewsbury Road. This case featured one of the young Hughes:

MISCHIEVOUS URCHINS.–At the Borough Police Court, six young urchins, whose heads scarcely appeared above the bar, were charged with making a fire in a building belonging to Messrs Morris, builders, in Salop Road. It appeared that one of the boys bought a "hapeath" of matches, while another struck a light, and the third ignited a quantity of straw which had been placed beneath a plank. Fortunately, the fire was discovered almost immediately after its commencement, or the building, which contained a large quantity of timber, would probably have been destroyed. The mayor gave the boys some kindly advice, and dismissed them. The names included D. Hughes (of the race of Bunter).
January 7, 1863

This featured the highway robbery Bunter; he was obviously used to being in gaol:

John Hughes, better known as "Bunter," was charged with stealing a set of fleams [*a fleam was a knife used in surgery or slaughtering*], of the value of 1 shilling, from the slaughterhouse of John Jones, butcher. The case was remanded in consequence of the absence of a material witness. Bunter expressed a wish to be sent to Shrewsbury, because he wanted warmer quarters than the Oswestry cells, where he suffered from the cold.
January 21, 1863

There was much discussion about the lack of a public hall in Oswestry, and now something was being done about it:

A public meeting was held at the Guildhall, on Friday evening, for the purpose of promoting the erection of a Public Hall, and the establishment of a Literary Institute for the town of Oswestry.
January 28, 1863

This bellman was not the drunk one from 1855, but the one who came before and after him:

DEATH OF THE BELLMAN.–The past week has carried off William Davies, the old bellman. The deceased had served in several excellent situations during his eventful life. He followed the fortunes of more than one master abroad. He was under-butler to Lord Cardigan; and, later still, we believe, he was in the service of an Irish bishop. Davis came to Oswestry some years ago, to reside with his sister at the Oak Inn, and was shortly afterwards

appointed bellman. In those days newspapers and expeditious printing had not ruined the office, but of late we fancy the chief emolument from the situation was the annual suit of gaudy livery given by the Mayor.
February 4, 1863

There was not a single murder reported in the town of Oswestry for the years of this book; but there were a few in the area, including this one in Baschurch, where a man killed his young disabled son:

The particulars of a most cold-blooded murder at Baschurch, will be read with feelings of sorrow by the people of our district. A man named Edward Cooper, a farm labourer, is a widower, and had two children, a girl of six and a boy between eight and nine years of age, a poor miserable cripple – hump-backed, and pigeon-breasted. The girl he placed in the care of a woman; and the boy at the house of a labourer at Frankton.

Cooper could not look after his children, because as a labourer on a farm there was nowhere for them to stay. Forced to have the boy back, he put him in the loft of the farmer's stable. The farmer's wife, Mrs Lewis, found the boy there, and sent him food, but of course he could not stay. Cooper visited relatives to try and place the boy:

Cooper took the boy to Hanwood, and did not return until Monday, when he told Mrs Lewis that he had met with a cousin who had taken the boy to Manchester. Cooper left the neighbourhood, and suspicious rumours were speedily afloat, and Mr Superintendent Ivins and his men made sundry investigations.

They discovered that Cooper, on his way back from Hanwood to Baschurch, had called at a cottage and borrowed a spade. They searched a wood near the cottage, and found the body of the child in a recently dug hole. Edward Cooper was arrested, brought for trial, and convicted. After the trial he made a full confession:

"When my wife died she wished me to be married again, so as to keep the home for my two children. I took a liking to a girl at Mr Wolryche's, Jane Saddler. She had promised to marry, but Mr Wolryche persuaded her to stop in his service, and that prevented the marriage that time. She had been very kind to the children after my wife's death."

It seems it was desperately difficult for him, alone with two young children, and he wasn't allowed a cottage as he wasn't married. Now Jane Saddler said she wouldn't marry him he didn't know what to do with his boy. The various relatives in Hanwood wouldn't look after the boy, so he and the child went back towards Baschurch, and went into a wood:

"I went into the coppice to catch rabbits. I did not catch any. I was in the coppice about half an hour before I went for the spade. I had no intention of doing anything to my little boy till I was in the coppice. The boy was sometimes with me, sometimes hunting about in the coppice.
I don't know what came over my mind, but I made away with the child. It was done with a handkerchief he had on. I tied the handkerchief tighter.

I seized him; his back was to me. It came over my mind as if I could not control myself. I left him there. As soon as the boy was dead I went for the spade; he was quite dead when I put him into the hole. My poor boy was a sharp boy; he could not read or write; he had done nothing to vex me, and I cannot tell what came over my mind at the time.

I feel very sorry from my own heart that I brought myself to this destruction that I have; and I am thankful that God Almighty has allowed me such a length of time to prepare for another world; and I hope He will have mercy on my little girl."

The case is dreadfully sad, a man driven to despair by poverty and circumstances murders his child, but he was sentenced to death, and executed before a large crowd in Shrewsbury (public hangings ceased five years later). The Advertiser had a grim description of the people who came for the entertainment of watching him hang:

The last act in the sad tragedy was performed on Saturday, and the wretched man, Edward Cooper, was 'hanged by the neck until he was dead,' in front of Shrewsbury gaol, in the presence of many thousands of heartless, or morbid, or ribald, or dishonest, or otherwise wrong-minded people. We cannot let the occasion pass without asking why the terrors of the law should not be executed inside the prison walls, before a few constituted authorities, rather than outside, before the scum of the nation, whose ribald jests and unblushing villainy runs riot in the midst of the most solemn moments of a fellow creature's history, when the wretched sinner, in his agony is launched into eternity.

From an early hour in the morning, people arrived and took up their stand at the best available points for gaining a sight of the fatal drop. Along in front of the gaol to the railway wall, down Howard-street, to the very edge of the Severn, vast crowds had collected, and on every available place and eminence commanding a sight of the scaffold, people were perched as thickly as crows in a densely-populated rookery.

March 4 & April 15, 1863

The Post Office seems to have moved location frequently:

Most of our readers know by this time that the Post Office has been removed from Willow-street to the passage leading from Church-street to the Smithfield. If the Post Office authorities wanted to place the office in as inconvenient position as possible, they could scarcely have accomplished their object better.

March 18, 1863

This is another case of a young boy being badly bullied:

John Castole, was charged with assaulting a boy named Williams, ten years old, who appeared with his head bandaged up.

The little boy said: I lodge in Bailey-street. I was out yesterday, with my brother, and when I returned I found the defendant in the house. Defendant lodges at the same place as my father and mother. Defendant sent me out for a candle. I went for it, and when I returned he said, "so help me God, if I do not make you lie in your bed before you go to sleep tonight," and then he struck me. He did so because there was no fire for him when he came home. I knelt down to light the fire, and he struck me three times–once with the tongs. He hurt me very much. I did not know there was a hole in my head until I put my finger in it.

The man said he only slapped the boy lightly on the side of the head.
March 11, 1863

One of the dangers of having to drive cattle through the town is illustrated here:

A WILD COW.–On Monday evening, a cow belonging to Mr Jackson the butcher, which was being driven through the town, rushed at several persons on Albion Hill, and injured some of them, not seriously. The animal then proceeded towards the Horse Market, where it jumped over a wall and rushed at a man who was on the other side. From there the cow made its way to a lane in the direction of Selattyn, where barricades were erected; and the next morning the animal was driven to the town quietly enough, and killed.
March 25, 1863

Another Bunter case, with his friend providing a very convincing excuse (unless the date is significant):

George Hughes (the original Bunter), who did not appear, and John Halliday, were charged with fighting in Beatrice-street.

Halliday–I was fighting, but I hope you will take it into consideration that though it was not the marriage day of the Prince of Wales and the Princess Alexandra, still it was a kind of rejoicing, for the town was illuminated. And I feel confident that had I not been drunk there would have been no disturbance as far as I was concerned.
April 1, 1863

Frequently neighbours had battles with each other, as they do now:

Mary Jones, of the White Horse, was charged with assaulting Sarah Jones, wife of John Jones, Butcher.

Complainant said the defendant placed a brick in the yard so as to prevent the water from running, so that the yard was filled with water. Complainant went to remove the brick, and defendant looked at her and said, "will you?" Defendant then removed the brick, and immediately afterwards a brick came over a wall and onto her head, "which bled profusely." She did not see any one throwing a brick but she had no doubt that defendant threw it.

Complainant's servant said she saw defendant taking up a brick, and then saw a brick coming over the wall.

Mrs Hollis heard defendant saying she would kill complainant before she died.

Mr Cartwright [*the magistrate*]–Two Mrs Jones's: we consider this a most disgraceful transaction, and dismiss the case. Your husbands ought to settle the dispute.
April 1, 1863

This fire turns out to be quite minor, compared to others in the town:

A NARROW ESCAPE.–On Sunday evening last, between eight and nine o'clock, the inhabitants of the town were alarmed by a cry of "Fire." It was soon discovered that the cause of the alarm was the smoke was issuing from the seed warehouse occupied by Mr Weaver, in Bailey-street. The small fire engine "The Fury," was quickly brought to the place, where a large crowd had gathered in a very few minutes. Everything was got into working order and a door at the warehouse was opened, but it was soon found that the services of the fire engine would not be required, as a few buckets of water sufficed to extinguish the smouldering fire.
April 22, 1863

Though this letter made a pertinent point:

SIR,–The recent fire in Bailey-street demonstrates the desirability of speedily providing waterworks for Oswestry. I hope the Town Council will take the subject into their serious consideration on Thursday.
Yours truly, A. B.
April 29, 1863

The Advertiser underlined the point, because having a waterworks influenced the siting of the railway works, which were so important to the growth of the town:

The attention of the inhabitants of Oswestry has recently been called to two questions of very great importance to the interests of the town–the probable erection of railway workshops, which would benefit trade more largely, perhaps, than most of our readers suppose, and the desirability of providing waterworks, for the comfort and health of the inhabitants. We are now informed, on the very best authority, that one of these schemes is in some degree dependent on the other–at any rate, that the former would at once be commenced with vigour, were there any definite plan of the latter before the public. We believe we are correct in stating that, according to the present plans, it is Mr Savin's intention to spend something like £25,000 on the new workshops, and that he is anxious to commence in erecting them as soon as possible.
May 6, 1863

This couple seems to have needed more than counselling to help their marriage:

MATRIMONIAL BLISS.–Thomas Parry was charged with assaulting his wife Mary Ann Parry, in the parish of Oswestry. Upon being asked whether he assaulted her, defendant (flourishing a stick) said–I did. (Laughter.) This is what I did it with. (Laughter.) I told her five dozen times not to do it, and then I laid this stick on her back, between light and heavy. (Laughter.)

The court (to complainant)–How long have you been married?

Complainant [*the husband*]–Five years.

Defendant [*the wife*]–Come August; and that is five years too much. (Laughter.)

Complainant–I want apart from him; one for one way and one another. (Laughter.)

The defendant produced a piece of cheese, saying–This is what she placed on the table for my breakfast. It is not fit for dogs. Will you please to smell him? (Laughter.)

The court refused to do so.

May 6, 1863

One of Savin's schemes was to get people to spend day trips on the west Wales coast:

TEN HOURS AT THE SEASIDE.– The line from Machynlleth to Borth (a beautiful bathing place) will shortly be open, and Messrs Savin and Ward intend issuing day tickets at a trifling cost, and so arranging the trains that a long day may be spent at the seashore.

June 3, 1863

Cambrian Hotel, Borth.

One of Savin's huge hotels, the Cambrian, in Borth, as advertised in the Advertiser; another of his hotels was the sandstone neo-Gothic building in Aberystwyth that is now known as the 'Old-College'

The Bunters seemed to feel persecuted:

Richard Powell and George Hughes, one of the race of "Bunter," were charged with fighting.

Police Constable Lloyd deposed that he found the defendants fighting by the Cross Keys. Hughes was stripped, but Powell was not. There was a great noise, and a great crowd was collected; and both men were drunk.

Hughes–If you heard a fight from the top of Church-street, you would say that Bunter was in it.

Fined £1, including costs; in default, fourteen days.

Powell–We shall go to gaol.

Hughes–If there's a fight and the policeman's a mile away, he says Bunter's in it.

June 3, 1863

On an important day for the local railways, all the companies were to be joined into one famous company:

A bill was promoted by the Oswestry and Newtown, the Llanidloes and Newtown, the Oswestry, Ellesmere, and Whitchurch, and the Newtown and Machynlleth companies, for the amalgamation of those four companies into one, under the name of "The Cambrian Railways Company."

June 10, 1863

The county police force seems to have been an improvement on the town one:

It is gratifying to record that the number of cases brought before the magistrates during the past quarter was smaller than usual. The Recorder took occasion to compliment the police, by remarking that very few persons were arrested against whom no charge could be proved, and that, in all probability, no charge was improperly laid against anyone. Altogether, we think the town may be congratulated on the efficiency of its police force.

June 24, 1863

At last something was to be done about having a waterworks, with some famous Oswestry names on the committee:

The business of the meeting was commenced by long conversation as to the supply of water for the town. Several propositions were discussed,–which resulted in a motion being proposed by Mr Alderman Morris, and seconded by Mr Alderman Cartwright,–that the mayor, Mr T Minshall, Mr Savin, Mr Hilditch, and Mr G Owen, be a committee to make enquiries as to the cost of the works, and obtain other information as to the carrying out of waterworks.

September 2, 1863

Another reason not to get drunk:

HUSBAND AND WIFE.–In one case, where the summons had not yet been served, it was stated that the complainant took out a summons against his wife, but as he carried it home he got drunk, and his wife stole it from him!

September 30, 1863

There was a slight earthquake felt in the district. Perhaps this could be said about people's reaction now:

> It is somewhat curious to discover the very large number of persons who had felt the earthquake of Tuesday morning, when you talk to them on Wednesday, who knew nothing about it until they saw the newspapers of Wednesday morning!
>
> *October 14, 1863*

This is one of the first references to an area that concerned the town for a long time, the district known as New Town – around Castle Fields. The Rope Walk, owned by Thomas McKiernin, was between Albert Road and Castle Street, a long straight valley where rope could be stretched out to dry; a rickety bridge crossed it:

> DEAR SIR. –Many of our townsmen only know from hearsay that there is a 'quarter' newly added unto Oswestry, which has not yet received a proper name at the hands of the Corporation, but which is severally known as 'New Zealand,' 'Little Newtown,' 'Birkenhead,' &c. A dirtier place does not exist, although all the houses are new. A glimpse of the state of the pathways may be gained from Beatrice-street, but, dirty as is the road there, it is nothing to what is to be found by the venturous traveller who explores further on. Crossing the Rope-walk from this cluster of houses the people have to force their way knee-deep in mud; and if they step on one side to escape a pitfall at the end of the bridge, they stand a chance of being precipitated down the steep bank amongst Mr McKiernin's ropes. Rates are paid by the owners of property in this mud hole, but they have not yet been favoured by the introduction of gas, and now that the 'dark days before Christmas' are approaching, the women and children of the unhappy valley must consider themselves prisoners as soon as the shades of evening close over it. Have not our Corporation the power to mend (or rather make) roads in this locality; and should they not place there lamps? Yours, &c, Stick-in-the-Mud.
>
> *October 21, 1863*

MARRIAGE OF THE HONOURABLE LLOYD KENYON AND MISS ORMSBY-GORE.

'An announcement of the marriage of The Hon Lloyd Kenyon, eldest son of Lord Kenyon, of Gredington, who is to marry the only daughter of Mr Ralph Ormsby Gore, MP.' July 15, 1863

There was yet another triumph for Thomas Savin:

At the annual meeting of the Oswestry Town Council, on Mon-

day, Mr Savin was elected Mayor for the ensuing year. Everybody felt that if the office of Mayor conferred any honour upon the person selected to discharge its duties, Mr Savin was fully entitled to have that honour conferred upon him by the town of which, in the words of his proposer, Mr Longueville, he is "unquestionably the greatest benefactor."
November 11, 1863

Obviously some parts of town were less well looked after than others:

THE STREETS.–Mr Bickerton called attention to the dirty state of Beatrice-street below the Plough, and said some of the inhabitants, who were determined to stand this state of things no longer, wanted to know whether they could clean the street themselves, and stop the rate. They did not know whether the street had been swept this year!
November 25, 1863

This lad, led on by his friend, was severely punished:

SMOKING NOW-A-DAYS.–A YOUNG THIEF.–Thomas Jones, of Oswestry, a boy eleven years of age, was charged with stealing seven ounces of tobacco, the property of the Great Western Railway Company. A porter named Ellis stated that the prisoner was the son of David Jones, who is employed by Mr Jackson, carrier for the company. Witness saw prisoner in the goods warehouse, and he said he was waiting for his father. About ten minutes afterwards witness saw him leaning on a box and taking some tobacco out of a bag that was lying against the box, and put it in his pocket.

When the porter looked in the boy's pocket, he found the tobacco.

The boy began to cry and said he would not do it again. The boy pleaded guilty.–Sentenced to be confined for the remainder of the day and once whipped with nine strokes of a birch rod.
November 25, 1863

This is another meteorological account:

THE GALE.–The gale which blew with almost unparalleled violence in some parts of the country, on Thursday last, does not seem to have visited this district quite so furiously as many others. Here, however, the effects of the gale were observable in various ways. Early in the morning, part of a chimney fell at the Cross Keys, in Leg-street. A man, who was passing at the time, narrowly escaped the shower of bricks, which so terrified him that he took to his heels and ran–we should not like to say how far or how long. At the Old Chapel House a chimney was blown down and fell through the roof into one of the rooms; fortunately the house is at present unoccupied. In Llwyn Lane a portion of one of the walls of a new house, which is in course of erection there, was blown down by the violence of the gale. We have heard of no serious casualties in this neighbourhood.
December 9, 1863

There was another fire in Oswestry:

FIRE IN WILLOW-STREET.–On Wednesday evening, between six and seven o'clock, a fire took place at Mr Parry's tan yard in Willow-street. The fire is supposed to have been caused by the overheating of a kiln beneath a drying room in which a considerable quantity of wool was lying. A large crowd soon collected, and the fire engines were speedily brought to bear upon the flames. Through the exertions of the firemen and others, the flames were soon extinguished.
February 3, 1864

This story of the death of Joseph Garrett showed the danger of excessive drinking:

Mrs Garrett, the wife of deceased, said–I was woken early in the morning by my husband. It was about 4:30 o'clock. He told me that something had struck him. He said, it is like fire in my head; and then he got up and said it had gone into his legs. He said some other things, and then I said to him–"You are not right, you have got the horrors of drink on you." He replied he was right enough. He had great difficulty in bringing his words out properly. He fell down, and then got up again, and leaned his head against the bed. He used to drink whiskey and beer. He was drunk on Monday night and on Saturday night, and he was drunk on Wednesday night. He used to get drunk sometimes every night. Sometimes he had fits when in drink. He was thirty-seven years old.
The jury thought the evidence was very plain, and brought in the verdict, "Died of apoplexy, brought on by excessive drinking."
At the close of the inquest, Mr Griffiths [*the doctor*] said the air of the house in which deceased had died was most impure and unhealthy, owing to the smoke in the room. It was so bad that he had no doubt it tended to hasten the death of deceased. –Several of the jury also spoke of the unhealthiness of the house, owing to the dirty state it was in and to the number of the families living (or rather existing) in it.
February 3, 1864

This was a proud report from the still expanding Advertiser:

The present issue of *The Advertiser* is the first printed sheet ever produced by steam power in Oswestry. It is not our usual practice to boast of our circulation, but we may observe that this week we issue Three Thousand Five Hundred copies of our paper,–a number, we have reason to believe, not exceeding–if indeed equalled–by any newspaper in Shropshire or North Wales; and a number six times as great as that of some of our contemporaries.
March 2, 1864

There was a battle for control of the newly amalgamated Cambrian Railways, and the Advertiser was of course on the side of Thomas Savin, because he wanted the Cambrian Railway works to be in Oswestry:

> Under the impression that the permanent works would be erected here, many persons have built new houses, and others have laid foundations; and if, after all, the works are not to remain in the town, many of these buildings will degenerate in value, and, in some cases, we fear, the owners– who are poor men, and have borrowed money to build–will be seriously injured. There is more probability of the works remaining at Oswestry whilst the affairs of the company are in the hands of Mr Savin. It is no new fact to state that the Board always wished to have the works at Moat Lane [*near Caersws*]. So Oswestry, whatever turn affairs take, will do well to support Mr Savin.
> *March 2, 1864*

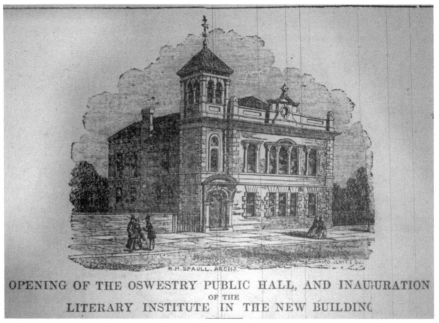

OPENING OF THE OSWESTRY PUBLIC HALL, AND INAUGURATION
OF THE
LITERARY INSTITUTE IN THE NEW BUILDING

There were no public halls in Oswestry in 1863. In 1864 two were built. The first was on the road leading to the railway station, announced on May 4, 1864.

There was still little progress on a waterworks:

> Last week, a correspondent, well qualified to speak upon the subject, urged the desirability of at once adopting the necessary steps for constructing water works in the town of Oswestry. Tomorrow the quarterly meeting of the Council takes place, and then, we hope, the matter will be earnestly considered, and some practical measures adopted for promoting this very

important subject. Otherwise, we are sure the inhabitants of Oswestry will be greatly disappointed.
May 25, 1864

Clawddu (between Bailey Street and Willow Street) was not a healthy place:

Sir,–Will you kindly give my letter a space in your widely circulated paper, that it may catch the eye of someone of the (seemingly blind) health committee of this pushing little town of Oswestry. That they may open their eyes and hearts (if they have any) to expend a trifling sum to remove one of the greatest nuisances in one of the principal thoroughfares in town. That is, the stench arising from stagnant water in the would-be channel of Market-street, better known as the Clawddu. I would ask one of that said committee to walk from Paris House corner to the market doors, and ask yourself the question, what is this strange smell? Does this strange smell proceed from an unknown cause? Let him look down, and he will find that every house has to throw its refuse to the front. They may scrub–they may brush–they may swill–until they scrape up the dry stones, and still there is such a stench that the very dogs run faster through this place of filth than any other part of the town. I honestly assert that I have seen people on market days black in the face with holding their breath while passing. Yours, &c. A Victim, But a Lover of Health.
May 25, 1864

News was travelling faster:

The Telegraph and the Press.–As an instance of the rapidity with which intelligence is circulated nowadays, through the agency of the telegraph and the printing press, it may be mentioned that nineteen minutes after the Derby was run at Epsom, on Wednesday, the names of the three first horses were posted in the streets of Oswestry.
June 1, 1864

After the wild cow in the streets in the previous year, here is something a little less usual for Shropshire:

A leopard loose.–Last week, as some of our readers know, Wombwell's menagerie visited this town, and took up its quarters at the White Lion Croft, Willow-street. On Thursday morning, previously to their departure, the men were repairing a van in which a leopard was confined, and left their work for a little while, for breakfast, we believe. During the absence of the men, the leopard made his escape from the van, and proceeded to the garden at the back of Porkington Terrace, where some of the inhabitants were naturally not a little alarmed at the appearance of so formidable beast. The keepers were communicated with, and the leopard, who did not seem to betray any signs of his savage tastes, was taken back to the van.
June 8, 1864

This is a rare phenomenon:

> STRANGE FREAK OF LIGHTNING.–On Sunday afternoon, about five o'clock, a thunderstorm passed over this town, and a very strange phenomenon was witnessed at one of the houses in Church-street. A lady, who was sitting in the parlour, saw the lightning, as it were, coming down the chimney, sweeping over the fire irons, and then playing, for a moment or two, about her dress. The servant boy, who was sitting in the kitchen at the time, seeing a light in the parlour, rushed in, under the apprehension that the lady was in flames! Happily, the lady was wearing a silk dress, which perhaps protected her from injury.
> June 8, 1864

There was a bridge over the Rope Walk, that linked Castle Street and Albert Road, and it was clearly very dangerous:

> SIR,–I should be glad to know, and perhaps you can inform me, who are the parties legally responsible for the safety of this elegant though frail structure. It cannot be the authorities of the neighbouring town of Oswestry, for I have been told that these gentlemen have satisfactorily proved that beyond directing their rate collector to call on the inhabitants four times a year for a certain amount of the circulating medium, they have no further duties to perform in the district referred to.
> Yours, &c., WHO'S TO BLAME? Noman's land, near Oswestry,
> June 29, 1864

This announcement meant that Oswestry would change dramatically:

> The announcement that the Cambrian company have decided on the site for their workshops, and that Oswestry is the place chosen, will be received with many manifestations of delight in the district. We understand that Mr George Owen, the engineer to the company, Mr John Ward, contractor, and one or two others, will meet on Friday next, to lay out the land for the buildings, which are to be erected on the recently levelled ground in the Shelf field.
> August 17, 1864

But the prospects for a waterworks had less success, as can be seen from this letter:

> A WAGER.–Mr BROWN and Mr JONES, meeting in Bailey-street, on Monday last, the following conversation ensues:–
> Brown–'The Council meet again this morning on the Waterworks question; bet you two to one in shillings they refer the matter to a committee.' Jones–
> 'Done, they do not, they will adjourn.'

(Robinson, a councilman, is seen advancing.) *Brown*–'Here is Robinson, let us appeal to him." (The question is put.) *Robinson*–'We met and talked on several matters, but everything was adjourned.' *Jones* (to Brown)–'Tip us the blunt.' *Brown* (handing it)–'At any rate, it was as usual–THEY DID NOTHING!'
August 17, 1864

Though, at that adjourned meeting of the Oswestry Town Council, some progress was made in the matter of the waterworks, and a related matter was mentioned, that of sewerage:

Engineers were appointed to survey the district and report to the Council upon the best method of obtaining a water supply. In the course of the discussion Mr Cartwright referred to the necessity for draining the town of Oswestry as quite as great as the need of waterworks. At present, strangers visiting Oswestry are disgusted with the nuisances which are bound so largely in the shape of offensive smells and open cesspools, and surprised at the apathy of the inhabitants who are content to live quietly and unresistingly in the midst of all these abominations. We trust that we shall soon see Oswestry rescued from its present position of being the town of many smells.
August 31, 1864

The rumours were more dramatic than the truth here, though there could have been serious consequences:

FALL OF A HOUSE.–On Thursday afternoon the inhabitants of Oswestry were thrown into a state of some excitement by the report that an inhabited house in Beatrice-street had fallen, and that a workman employed in digging the foundation of a neighbouring house was seriously, if not fatally, injured. A large crowd soon collected at the scene of the disaster near the turnpike gate, when it was discovered, as usual, that the report was somewhat exaggerated. Part of one of the new houses, however, had fallen, and two workmen were injured, one of them rather severely. The house was one of three, and the part which fell consisted of the end nearest the turnpike gate. The excavations for the foundations of the new houses appear to have approached too near the walls of the passage, which consequently fell, carrying with it the part of the adjoining house, one of the bedrooms of which is exposed to public view. In this bedroom a child was sleeping at the time of the accident, but happily at the further end which remained standing.
September 7, 1864

Oswestry had more than one reason to be 'the town of many smells':

DEAR SIR,–My stomach was very much out of order last Friday morning, owing to a dreadful nuisance. I think some men were carrying manure out of an entry situate about half way down Bailey-street, and depositing it in the street. I could even perceive the stench although some distance away, but I very much pity those people living close by. This is not the first time I have smelt this unpleasant odour, I think it always comes from the same street.

By inserting this in your next number you will greatly oblige your old friend, BAILEY PUMP.
September 14, 1864

This is a truly appalling case with pitiful consequences – for bagpipes:

ASSAULT AND ROBBERY.–Late on Saturday night, as a well-known piper, living in Beatrice-street, was coming from Carneddau to Oswestry, he was attacked somewhere on the road and robbed of his knife, his bagpipes at the same time being smashed to pieces. He was dreadfully abused about the head, but was so drunk that he can give the police no reliable information on the subject.
September 21, 1864

Another murder, and again of a son killed by his father, happened in Llanymynech:

It appears that a rockman, David Davies, had, residing under his roof, a son, James Davies, thirty years of age, of violent and ungovernable temper, and frequent quarrels took place. The other day the father and son quarrelled over their work, and the latter irritated the old man to such a degree, he raised a stone and dashed it at him; and, in consequence of the blow, the son died.

David Davies was committed for trial for manslaughter at the Montgomeryshire Assizes. In March 1865:

The jury returned a verdict of guilty, and prisoner was sentenced to two months' hard labour.
September 21, 1864 & March 15, 1865

The second public hall to be opened in Oswestry was the Victoria Rooms:

OPENING OF THE VICTORIA ROOMS.
"These rooms," which "have been instructed for large assemblies, for agricultural meetings and flower shows, for balls, concerts, and select entertainments, and for lectures of a scientific and instructive character" (to quote from the prospectus), were opened with great eclat last Thursday.
September 21, 1864

LEA AND PERRINS' CELEBRATED

WORCESTERSHIRE SAUCE.

THE GREAT SUCCESS of this DELICIOUS CONDIMENT has been the signal for the appearance of many SPURIOUS IMITATIONS totally different in FLAVOR and destitute of the DIGESTIVE PROPERTIES of this SAUCE.

Purchasers are earnestly requested to
ASK FOR LEA & PERRINS' SAUCE,
Prepared only by
LEA & PERRINS, Worcester.

*⁎*Sold Wholesale and for Export, by CROSSE & BLACKWELL, London, and all Merchants and Oilmen.

There was progress on the Oswestry waterworks, again thanks to Mr Savin's energy. Pen-y-gwely reservoir is above Rhydycroesau:

> Messrs Gotto and Beesley have presented their report, which the Council, or rather the Local Board, have duly considered, and upon which they have taken action. The engineers have turned their attention to Penyg-welley Brook, and it is from that stream mainly, if not entirely, we expect, that the town will be supplied with water. In the dry season, when the gaugings were made, the quantity of water flowing was 239,000 gallons in twenty-four hours, and that quantity would be largely increased in wet weather and during the winter months.
>
> *October 12, 1864*

This is a very strange case, because it came to court, but was then dropped, probably because of threats made against the complainant. These days it's difficult to imagine that nothing more was done:

> SENDING A THREATENING LETTER.–Mary Ann Jones was charged with sending a threatening letter through the post to Mr William Merrick, Llys Lane, on Monday morning. Mr Merrick said–The letter produced I received from the postman on Monday morning, requesting me to attend in the Llys Lane at seven o'clock p.m., and to bring some money with me. In consequence I communicated with the police, and an arrangement was made at the time stated for me to attend. The prisoner met me in the Llys Lane at the time appointed, and she said "I have come to protect you." I then gave the signal and Sergeant Duncan came out from Mr Savin's premises and took her into custody.
>
> P.S. Duncan said–The prisoner said, "I have got no weapons about me; I came to beg his pardon." I took her in custody on the charge of sending a threatening letter for the purpose of extorting money. She afterwards told me that Mr Merrick had refused to lend her money on a policy and that she wanted to threaten him to induce him to give her money, so that she might go to her husband in America.

The case was adjourned, and when it came up again Mr Merrick didn't appear, frightened away. The extremely long and very threatening letter, presumably written by Mrs Jones's husband, was read out. This is just a small part of it:

> "You are alive yet, but not for long, unless you keep silent. Mind not a word, or a bullet will go through your head first thing. My wife wants seventy pounds, and unless you lend it to her, your days will be numbered. I was with her last night, and heard you refuse her. You said you had not got it. Now, that was a lie–I know what money and property you have got. Mind, you cannot deceive me, but I would tell you two parties have got me £100 to put you out of the way, and I would have done it before had not that woman prevented me. She begged me to spare your life; so I said I would on condition that you would give me seventy pounds, but not without, mind–not without. Now, I will make an agreement with you. If

you will give her the money, you may rest content, not a hair of your head shall be touched, and I will guard you from all your enemies in town–that or death. If you do not come and bring the money, you will not see tomorrow. I will do what I have been paid for–blow your brains out and set fire to your houses. You shall not live another day. People have been about your house at night for many weeks, but I have kept them off on purpose to give you a chance to live. Do not you think your life is worth more than seventy pounds? Another thing I will tell you. If you breathe a word of this to any living soul before you pay the money, I will dig my knife into your heart. I will be at your house tomorrow as soon as the postman. I will watch your every move and follow your every footstep all day until seven at night, with my pistol in hand; and should you breathe a word I will put a bullet through your head; and when you come at seven o'clock, you bring anyone along with you, my wife will not see you, and I will put you fast in the net when you do not expect it, and lay your grey head low for you."
November 16, 1864

Captain Dod was famous as the compiler of the 'Parliamentary Companion':

ACCIDENT TO CAPTAIN DOD.–We regret to hear that a serious accident happened to Captain Dod, of Nant Issa, near Oswestry, on Thursday last, while out shooting with a party from Mr Barnes's, M.P., of The Quinta. While the stock was under Captain Dod's armpit, and the muzzle pointing towards the ground, the charge of his gun exploded, and the whole of it entered Captain Dod's right ankle and foot. Captain Dod was conveyed home by the whole of the party. So much damage had been done that amputation was decided on, and performed next morning, halfway up the lower leg. Up to the present time the patient is doing as well as can be expected after so severe an accident.
December 21, 1864

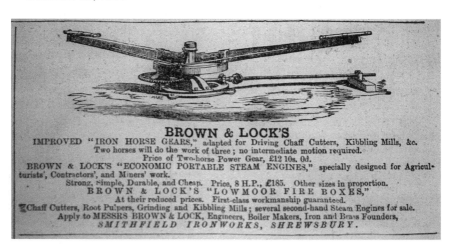

Early in the year the Advertiser summed up what 1864 had done for Oswestry, praising in particular the great Mr Savin:

> When the future historian comes to write a continuation of the records of Oswaldstre, from the date at which the existing histories break off, among the most eventful years will be the one which has just departed.
>
> First and foremost must be noted down completion of the railway system between the North of England and South Wales by means of the Oswestry and Ellesmere, and the Mid Wales Railway. Our town is now on what will one day doubtless become a most important main line, and Mr Savin is to be congratulated on the quiet progress the Ellesmere portion is making.
>
> But this completion of the system is by no means all the benefit Oswestry will gain from its railways. The huge workshops commenced during the year, and which are so rapidly rising on the Shelf bank field, hold out a glorious promise of future prosperity to the town. Mr Savin might, no doubt, have made a better bargain by placing these works elsewhere, but he shewed himself a true friend to his native parish, and built his workshops at Oswestry.
>
> *January 4, 1865*

In 1864 we left Captain Dod badly injured after shooting himself in the foot:

> One of the latest gun accidents has resulted in the death of the possessor of a widely known name–Captain Dod, compiler of the *Parliamentary Companion* and *Peerage*. Captain Dod was out shooting about a month ago, when his watchguard caught the trigger of his gun, the content of which were lodged in his foot. Amputation became necessary, intermittent fever set in, and last week Captain Dod sank under the shock to the system.
>
> *January 25, 1865*

Some criminal cases were treated amazingly leniently. These days this man would probably be locked up for several years:

> Thomas Evans, porter at the Cambrian Station, was charged with indecently assaulting Margaret Eliza Thomson, aged ten, the daughter of a signalman on the Cambrian Line. It appeared that prisoner lodged with the child's father, and took occasion of the parent's absence to commit the offence. The jury found the prisoner guilty of indecent assault, and in consideration of the good character given him, and a recommendation

The OSWESTRY ADVERTISER,
Montgomeryshire Mercury, North Shropshire Gazette, and Local Journal for the Borders of Wales.

to mercy on the part of the child's father, a sentence of only three weeks' hard labour was inflicted.
January 4, 1865

A warning was given about some rascally female travelling players:

SIR,– Last week a company of people calling themselves the Female Christy Minstrels visited Oswestry and gave an entertainment at the Public Hall. As certain facts had reached the ears of the hall keeper with reference to these persons, payment was demanded immediately at the close of the performance, and an attempt was made to detain the "properties." The "minstrels," however, displayed a dexterity which showed considerable practice, and managed to slip the bolts and escape with their goods, refusing, with the behaviour not the most refined, to pay a penny. I know that other accounts in the town were also left undischarged. I may add that when the hall was applied for, a respectable looking letter was written, saying the room was required for a "concert," and not further mentioning the nature of the performance.
February 8, 1865

VALENTINES! VALENTINES!!

The Attention of the public generally is invited to a very large assortment, just received from London. Such Elegant emblems of love and affection certainly could Not possibly be obtained except at this establishment. The prices being moderate, they are within the reach of all. In design they have been pronounced to be charming. Now is the time those wishing to give proof of their Endless affection, to inspect the extensive and beautiful STOCK,
AT
ASKEW ROBERTS'S,
Bailey Head, Oswestry.

This plea at a Town Council meeting would not be answered until 1923:

Mr Cartwright this week called attention to the great inconvenience which arises from the continued existence of two railway stations at Oswestry. Those who travel by the Great Western, through Oswestry, to Wales, will feel the force of his remarks. A change at Gobowen, a dilatory run of two miles, and then another and worse change at Oswestry, are a series of annoyances which travellers cannot be expected to submit, in these days, with perfect equanimity, especially when there is no good reason why they should be subjected to so much trouble.
February 15, 1865

This shows one particular policeman behaving in a very commendable way:

NEARLY LOST IN THE SNOW.–On Sunday night between seven and eight o'clock, an old man named Evan Davies, who is nearly eighty years of age, was walking from Chirk to Oswestry, and when a few yards from

Oakhurst found it impossible to proceed any further without assistance. Happily another man shortly came by, and promised to send assistance from Oswestry, and P.C.Jones accordingly went in search of the unfortunate pedestrian, who he found leaning against the wall and quite incapable of walking. P.C.Jones took the old man on his back and carried him all the way to Oswestry, where he was comfortably located in a lodging house. The old man said he was travelling from Liverpool to South Wales in search of his son, and had been all day long walking from Chirk.
February 15, 1865

This is the sad case of a young man called Jonah Jones, who cut his own throat:

Robert Jones, wheelwright, said–I live in Willow-street. Deceased was my brother. He would have been twenty-five in July. He was a labourer. I last saw him alive about a quarter past two yesterday afternoon, when he was in bed. His head seemed very queer and light. He appeared strange in his manner. He said he fancied he saw different things, he did not know what. He said my face looked different, as if it were of a green cast. Nothing seemed to be the right colour to him. About five months ago, as near as I can recollect, he was in the same way before. I have heard that two of my uncles were similarly affected. This was the third time deceased had been in that way. The time before this he used to make motions across his throat, and when he came to himself I asked what he meant by it. He said he fancied he saw people cutting their throats, and he felt bound to do the same thing. He said he felt the same when he heard a cow lowing. He was never in an asylum. My brother has had no quarrel with anyone. He was working in the same shop with me at Mr Windsor's.

The dead man seems to have been liked by everyone, but knowing he had suicidal tendencies tried to keep any shaving razors locked up. Unfortunately they were not successful:

William Mason, Shoemaker, Castle Fields, said–The deceased had lodged with me for about six months, and he was always a very sober, quiet, peaceable young man. I didn't see any change in him till Wednesday morning, when he seemed very low in spirits. I asked him was he not well, and he said, "no, I am not very well. I cannot go to my usual employment today." He said he could not come down to his breakfast as he was poorly, and I took him a cup of tea and toast, and he ate quite as heartily as usual. I fetched his brother, who came and said he would fetch the doctor, to which deceased replied, "very well." The brother fetched Mr Wynne. This was about three o'clock. I went up two or three times before five o'clock. I saw no difference in him; only he seemed very low. About a quarter to six we heard a noise as if he fell on the floor. I ran up as quickly as I could. I thought he was dead. I lifted his head, and found a terrible gash in his throat. I sent for his brother and Mr Wynne, and both were on the spot immediately. I did not see that deceased breathed at all after I went in.

There was a great quantity of blood about the floor. He was bleeding a little when I went in.

The coroner, in summing up, said there can be little doubt that the deceased destroyed himself in a fit of temporary insanity, and the jury returned a verdict to that effect.

April 26, 1865

We think of strikes as modern practices, but this one delayed the growth of the town, even if temporarily:

STRIKE IN THE BUILDING TRADE.—We are sorry to understand that in consequence of a strike in the building trade the many buildings now in course of erection in this town cannot be proceeded with. The men have struck for an increase in wages, but there is a probability of an early settlement of the dispute by the masters meeting the demand of the men half way.

May 3, 1865

The Advertiser reported 'The Terrible Railway Accident at Rednal'. This was on the GWR line, when an excursion train with an extraordinary 32 carriages went too fast over track that was being repaired. 13 people died, and 30 were badly injured. Many people seemed to have been responsible:

Now that the excitement has in some measure been allayed and the public having "supped full with horrors" provided for them by the newspapers, it will not be amiss to introduce our report of the inquest of the calm and sober outline of facts, as stated on oath before the coroner and jury.

The jury's verdict was: "We bring in a verdict of *Accidental Death*. We find that there was great blame attaching to the officials of the Great Western Company for not providing better brake power before leaving Chester, and in not providing better carriages and engines for the excursion train. We consider the enginemen guilty of gross and culpable negligence in not attending to the signal put up by the platelayers, and we believe the engines were going at too great a speed over a defective portion of the line, between Babbin's Wood bridge and the scene of the accident. We think the platelayers were also guilty of gross and culpable negligence in not properly and sufficiently packing the sleepers so as to make them

secure enough to bear so heavy a train as the excursion train, going at the rate the train was then going."
June 14, 1865

The chimney mentioned here still stands, on Gobowen Road:

THE RAILWAY WORKSHOPS.– On Wednesday night a flag was hoisted on the top of the chimney at these workshops, being the customary sign that the "rearing" was accomplished. The ceremony of breaking a bottle of wine at the top of the chimney was performed. The chimney is 150 feet high.
June 28, 1865

This letter comes from a time when outright sexism was not frowned on:

SIR,–The worst piece of news I have read in your paper is that the ladies have taken to canvassing. Ancient and modern writers have told us that they are at the bottom of all the mischief in the world, and upon my word, as far as my experience of life is gone, I really believe that. You are sitting in an armchair, quietly reading "The History of Woman." Suddenly
"By the simple opening of a door
All paradise lets itself in upon you."
There she stands radiant with smiles, and fragrant with goodness. You feel yourself under a shower of rainbow light, and all the sweetest influences of "Araby the Blest." A voice rings silvery on the ear, like the sound of an incense-tinkling bell–"Do promise me your vote!" While I look up, the look falls upon the floor–I hesitate, and gasp, and implore–just then a rosy finger gently touches my hand–and, oh sir, I must leave you to guess the rest, for I am ashamed to tell it.
Yours, WEAK AND PENITENT.
P.S.–Let it be known through your paper that every lady who asks for a vote must give a hearty kiss as the lowest price of it. I sold mine too cheaply.
June 28, 1865

There were more dangers than just bad smells in Oswestry. It was right to be afraid of cholera, as it is one of the most rapidly fatal illnesses known; infected people can die within three hours:

The Oswestry Local Board, roused up by the possible approach of cholera, have given strict orders to their inspector, to remove, as far as practicable, the many nuisances at present existing in what has rightly been called the "town of many smells." It is a nasty title, and by no means complimentary to the place; which certainly deserves it, however. Over and over again have we called attention to the shameful state of what might be the sweet and healthy little town of Oswestry. Blessed by nature beyond most other towns, it is yet a place from which people seeking pure air as well as beautiful scenery would certainly be driven away by the vile odours that would assail them on whichever side they attempted to enter it.
August 2, 1865

As expletives had to be deleted in the Advertiser, the effect of this case is lost:

Hannah Drury was charged with using abusive words towards Emma Jasper, at Oswestry. Complainant said defendant went up a yard on 8th of July, and called her all the —— and —— she could lay her tongue to. Not satisfied with that, she went up to complainant's door and called her a —— and ——, and other most offensive epithets.
August 2, 1865

In August came something farmers feared much more than Foot and Mouth disease – the Cattle Plague, or Rinderpest. Death rates among cattle are extremely high. The disease is mainly spread by direct contact and by drinking contaminated water, although it can also be transmitted by air:

The spread of the "cattle plague," and its appearance in, at least, one part of Shropshire, demand that immediate attention should be paid to the subject, by the agriculturists of this and the adjoining counties. In various counties, where the disease has not yet made its appearance, meetings have been held for the purpose of taking precautionary measures against it, and establishing Mutual Insurance Societies. Much more should the same plan be adopted in Shropshire, where the plague has already appeared.
August 16, 1865

There were not the same restrictions for dogs as now:

DANGEROUS DOGS.–The dangerous practice of allowing savage dogs to be at large was exemplified on Monday night, when Sergeant Duncan, who was on duty in the Cross, was severely bitten by a ferocious animal belonging to Mr Evans, the chemist.
August 23, 1865

It's questionable whether the medical men were entitled to be so certain of their opinion here:

A man named Pritchard, a member of the Rifle Corps, fired a blank cartridge at a man named Williams, to frighten him. The wound was severe enough to draw blood, and shortly afterwards the man died. An inquest was held, when it transpired from the evidence of the medical men,

that death was caused by effusion on the brain, brought on by excessive drinking, and was in no way to be attributed to the wound caused by the rifle or the shock consequent thereon. Nevertheless we would suggest that rifles are best kept in an armoury, and not within reach of the careless volunteer who would use so formidable a weapon in frolic.
August 30, 1865

A common complaint now is about roads being repaired, and then dug up again a short time later. This doesn't seem to be new, though in this case there seems to have been some undue influence from the MP's wife:

Mr Bickerton asked how it was that so much useless expense was now being thrown away on paving Willow-street. There were three men at work with a horse and cart, and there were several heaps of stones near the market. When the sewerage was done, that would all have to be done over again. Mr Spaull said the reason it was done was because Mrs Gore had complained of the state of the streets.
August 30, 1865

But at least in Oswestry the sewers were being put in and the waterworks built:

THE PUBLIC WORKS.–Our Oswestry readers will have observed with satisfaction how vigorously the contractors, Messrs Bugbird and Son, are pushing on the works. The sewers now being constructed in Leg-street, where, to save inconvenience to the shopkeepers by the accumulation of earth, the work is carried on by alternate excavating and tunnelling. The reservoirs at the old brick kilns near the Mount are also progressing satisfactorily. Some enquiries having been made as to why the sewerage and water pipes are not laid at the same time, we may state that the nature of the work rendered it simply impossible to carry on both operations with one cutting.
September 27, 1865

The Cattle Plague, so devastating to farmers, was getting nearer:

THE CATTLE PLAGUE.–It is with great regret we have to inform our readers that that awful calamity, the rinderpest, has come very close to our neighbourhood. Two cattle near Overton have been afflicted. Mr Roberts, veterinary surgeon of Oswestry, who has seen cases of the rinderpest in London, at once pronounced them as affected by the disease, and ordered them to be destroyed. They were killed and buried immediately.
October 4, 1865

To us this may appear to be a strange expression of snobbery:

It is proposed to establish in Shropshire a lunatic asylum for the middle and upper classes, who, at present, for the most part, are obliged to send their afflicted relations to private establishments. Though private establishments, on the whole, are conducted well, public asylums are not only much cheaper, but, what is of more importance, afford far better

guarantees that the patients are properly treated, both as far as skill and kindness are concerned.
October 18, 1865

The area around Castle Fields didn't seem to be improving:

THE STATE OF CASTLE FIELDS.–Mr Bailey said he begged to call attention to the state of Castle Fields. The roads were worse than a ploughed field, and the inhabitants had great difficulty in getting to their houses. People, who were not obliged to go there, no more thought of doing so than they would to a place infected by the plague.
December 6, 1865

Much of the Advertiser for this winter concerned the Cattle Plague:

CATTLE PLAGUE.–The magistrates have issued two orders, one prohibiting the bringing of any horned cattle, sheep, or pigs into the hundred of Oswestry up to the 1st of March next, and the other stopping the removal of animals for the purposes of sale to any place in the division, up to the same date.

The cattle plague is still spreading, and the accounts which we publish from places in our own district give good grounds for alarm. Indeed, bearing in mind that when the plague visited this country before it remained here for ten years, it is impossible to say for how long the public trade in cattle may be suspended.
December 6 & 13, 1865

The waterworks hadn't been finished, and there could hardly be a worse place than this for a fire:

FIRE.–On Saturday morning last, between two and three o'clock, an alarming fire broke out on the premises belonging to Messrs M Jones and son, chandlers [*candle makers*], Church-street. The fire was first discovered by Miss Corney, who immediately gave the alarm to Enoch Evans, nightwatchman on the sewerage works, who proceeded to Sergeant Duncan's, and three engines and firemen were quickly on the way. Notwithstanding the exertions of the fireman and others the whole of the melting house with its contents was entirely destroyed.
January 17, 1866

There was some hope that the cattle plague was not going to continue to spread:

The last cattle plague returns are more favourable, showing an increase of only 123, as compared with 1027 the week before. This apparently encouraging fact, however, may have little significance, since it has happened more than once other similar decrease in the returns has been followed by a corresponding increase. Still, we may hope that the practice of vaccination, which is spreading rapidly through the country, has something to do with the change.
January 24, 1866

The area of Castle Fields, sometimes known as New Town, had a nickname:

The Mayor of Oswestry has paid a visit to what was aptly termed by one of our correspondents, "the Dismal Swamp." The Dismal Swamp, otherwise called the New Town, is, like most disreputable persons and places, a thing of many affairs, and lies, as some of our Oswestry readers may know, just behind the Castle Bank. Into that dismal region, which the scavenger has never entered, and where gas-light is a thing only hinted at by the reflection of distant lamps, our worthy Mayor has penetrated, not, indeed, in disguise, because the darkness of the swamp is so intense that there was little danger of recognition at night time, when the expedition was made. From the expedition His Worship happily returned safely to civilised regions, and was able to give the Local Board on Monday the result of his experience. The conclusion at which he arrived, at which we have often tried to lead the authorities, is, that the new town is in a most disgraceful state, that it is a frightful place, and that women, if they value their safety, had better not venture within its limits. All this we have said over and over again.
January 31, 1866

The waterworks and sewerage were proceeding well:

OSWESTRY DRAINAGE WORKS.–The works for draining the town of Oswestry, and supplying it with water, which have been vigorously pushed forward during the last few months, are now about half completed. The water is brought from a distance of five miles. Rising amongst the hills, between the Lawnt and Llanarmon, some distance to the north of the Llanarmon Road, the Penygwelly brook only runs a short distance from the source before it is dammed up for the purposes of the waterworks. The pipes are then carried over the racecourse, as far as the old brick field opposite the Mount, where two ample reservoirs are constructed.

The sewage is to be carried from the town to a field near the Gallowstree Gate, between the Shrewsbury and Maesbury roads. From the character of the works, there is every reason to hope that when the sewerage is completed the inhabitants of Oswestry will be delivered from the many offensive smells by which they have suffered for so many years; and also that the agriculturists will be supplied with a cheap and efficacious manure.

January 31, 1866

Then, out of nowhere, came the first hint of the downfall of one of Oswestry's greatest men:

THE MONEY MARKET AND MR SAVIN.–The recent suspension of payment by Messrs J Watson and Co. caused many of the more thoughtful of the people of Wales to fear that the present state of the money market might seriously affect other contractors connected with the principality, and yesterday the money articles in the leading journals revealed the fact that Mr Savin, the largest, and the most enterprising of the whole, had been compelled to stop payment. A glance at the extract from the two best authorities on financial matters will show that Mr Savin's affairs are in by no means a bad position. Indeed with three millions of securities to meet two millions of debts, he is very clearly perfectly solvent; but in the present state of the Money Market, to realize would have been to sacrifice much; and Mr Savin has taken (as all who have the pleasure of knowing him

would readily support he would take,) the manly and honest course; that of placing himself in the hands of his creditors; so that they should be in a position to judge for themselves.
February 7, 1866

Unfortunately, despite the Advertiser's optimism, Savin was not 'perfectly solvent':

MR THOMAS SAVIN.–The fact that Mr Savin has been advised to place his affairs in the hands of his creditors is now known through the length and breadth of the land, and the more intelligent of the public know that these difficulties are only temporary; but there are still absurd rumours afloat and some people are even astonished that all the trains on the Cambrian system have not been stopped! It is useless to tell such as these that any men whose transactions in the money market or on some larger scale as those of Mr Savin must pass through critical times on their way to prosperity; any stoppage, in their eyes, means failure, and once payment is suspended, why there is an end of the business.
February 14, 1866

The Advertiser thought Savin's difficulties were temporary, but they weren't. His problem was that he had taken shares instead of money as payment for his railway building; and when the Aberdovey line proved to be expensive, he had no money to pay his creditors, and he was declared bankrupt. It was a sad end to an illustrious and meteoric career, from draper to great railway magnate in under ten years.

Nationally the cattle plague was taking its toll; this is a large number of dead cattle:

By the last official returns, the number of animals attacked in the week ending February 17 was 13,001. The number increases week by week, and a total of the cases reported since the appearance of the disease is now 166,379, of which 105,497 have died, and 19,227 have been killed; leaving 21,092 recoveries, and 20,563 beasts unaccounted for.
February 28, 1866

The improvements on the Castle Bank did not seem to last, mainly because it was being frequented by too many 'vagabonds and blacklegs':

SIR,–Will you allow me, through the medium of your valuable paper, to call attention to the disgraceful state of the Castle Hill, both as regards filth and the company who collect together on the top of it. It seems to be quite a deserted place as far as a keeper is concerned, and nobody seems to care what becomes of it.

A few summers ago it was nicely laid out with rose trees and flower beds, &c., whose fragrance gave the place a charm, but now it is a regular meeting place every Sunday evening for most of the young vagabonds and blacklegs of the town, who keep a continual uproar, with the most blasphemous language that can possibly be uttered.

I am, Sir, yours respectfully, OLD OSWESTRY.
April 4, 1866

The shed mentioned here is the station that was so ridiculed back in 1850, and at last it was replaced:

THE OLD STATION.–During the past week the shed which has served as the Great Western Railway Station for about sixteen years has been taken down, and a new station–a small, unpretentious brick building–is now in use.
April 11, 1866

This was an end to the hope that Oswestry would ever be on the Chester to Shrewsbury main line:

Our Oswestry readers will learn with regret that the Great Western Company have 'dropped' that portion of their bill before Parliament this year which would have conferred so great a boon upon Oswestry, and (as we believe) have been so lucrative to themselves. We refer to the new line to Rednal, by which the Gobowen branch would have been converted into a main line.
May 16, 1866

There was hope that the slum area of Oswestry was going to be improved:

THE NEW TOWN.–A "Voice from the Dismal Swamp" congratulates the inhabitants of the New Town that at last they have good prospect of better days. The sewerage works are progressing satisfactorily, and when they are completed, and the waterworks around it, with lighting and paving, the Dismal Swamp will begin to resemble an English town of the nineteenth century. The "voice" tells us of an old gentleman who, from living so long in those benighted regions beyond the Rope Walk, became a monomaniac, and persisted in asserting that the present occupier of the throne was Edward II. We do not wonder at it.
May 16, 1866

Even before the waterworks had been finished there were questions about its capacity:

WATER WORKS, BUT NO WATER.–A rumour has arisen, and it says Penygwelly has been dry, or all but dry, during the past week!–that the stream where (like a romantic young lady) it once was gushing, is now, like the oldest of sour old maids–But the simile is a dangerous one, and the subject is painful. Can you give your readers any definite information?
May 30, 1866

This Advertiser editorial attacked the patently absurd idea that women should be allowed to vote:

Mr [*John Stuart*] Mill, who has already appeared in his books as the advocate of a woman's franchise, has now carried his powerful advocacy into the very walls of Parliament. We neither believe nor hope that he will we successful. After all is said, there remains the eternal fact that women, if

they fulfil their proper social function, will scarcely ever be qualified by political knowledge, or mental impartiality, to exercise the privilege of voting. A woman who is worth anything, and yet is not one of the very highest of the human race, will vote from feeling rather than from thoughts, and help to introduce fresh complications into the arena of politics. If women really knew their own interests, and their own glory, they would be the first to deprecate any attempt to force them into the fierce political battle-field, since it is in far different, and in some senses higher, paths that their true duty lies.
June 20, 1866

The state of the roads was not improved by having pipes laid under them. Certainly Health and Safety was not much attended to:

ACCIDENTS.–On Friday, as a cart, loaded with bark, was passing along Beatrice-street, one of the wheels sank into a portion of the street which had been excavated for the sewerage works and recently filled up. Various appliances were brought to bear to extricate the wheel, but it was upwards of an hour before they succeeded.–In one or two places, during the week, children have fallen into the sewerage cuttings, but without sustaining any serious injuries. It is a matter for much congratulation that the carrying out the works, which are now nearly completed, has been unattended by any serious accidents.
June 27, 1866

This accident shows again the dangers of the horse and trap:

SAD AND DISTRESSING FATAL ACCIDENT.–It is our melancholy duty this day to record the death of Madame Donnez, a lady known to very many friends in Oswestry. The deceased lady was on a visit to Mr Septimus Edwards, a surgeon, and last Friday she accompanied him on his round of visits. While making a call one of his patients, he left the reins of the horses in Madame Donnez's hands, and during the time of his absence a sudden flash of lightning startled the horses, and so terrified them that they ran away. Madame Donnez was greatly alarmed, and attempted to jump out of the vehicle, but unhappily some portion of her dress caught as she did so, and she was dragged along for the distance of half a mile before the horses could be stopped. So terribly was the deceased lady injured that she lingered insensible for about two hours, and then died. Her mortal remains were interred yesterday in the Oswestry Cemetery.
July 11, 1866

The town gate at Beatrice Street was at the point where Castle Street meets Beatrice Street; according to Isaac Watkins, the pillars that replaced the gate, for the turnpike road, are now those at the entrance to the Castle Bank:

THE OLD TOWN GATES.–A correspondent writes to complain of the "act of Vandalism" which has taken place in Beatrice-street, where one of the

pillars of the old town gates has been removed. We should like to have an explanation of this.
July 18, 1866

Finally, the long expected waterworks were opened:

It is our refreshing duty, in this hot and dusty summer time, to chronicle the opening of the Oswestry waterworks, with a pleasant proceedings which took place at Penygwelly on Monday to commemorate the event.
The water and sewerage works have been completed at a total cost of about £207,000, which is very little in excess of the estimates. There are, altogether, eight miles of water pipes and five miles of sewerage pipes. The number of bricks used in the construction of the works is 630,000; 5000 joints have been made; the number of cubic feet of earthwork is 1,410,000; 600 tonnes of iron have

One of the turnpike gate pillars now at Castle Bank that used to be on Beatrice Street ('TOLL THOROUGH' is carved in the stone near the top)

been used, 19,000 lineal feet of deal, 4000 lineal feet of struts, and 12,000 square feet of elm timber. The works were commenced last September, and have therefore been completed in about ten months. The engineers are Messrs Gotto and Beesley of London.
July 18, 1866

Here is yet another case for Relate:

HUSBAND AND WIFE.–A DEPLORABLE CASE.–Edward Maddox, joiner, was charged with assaulting his wife, Elizabeth Maddox, on July 10.
Complainant said–I got into bed on the night in question and he abused me. I told him I would summon him, and next morning he got drunk before breakfast and came home and lay on the sofa. I told him he ought to go to work and tried to pull him up, and he then assaulted me. I only want you to make him allow me something to keep me and my children, and not to hurt him.
Defendant–I cannot live with her. She is a drunken woman. Did I not find you drunk at the George the other day, drinking with other men?
Complainant–It was you who taught me to drink, by bringing me beer before breakfast.

Defendant–I cannot live with a drunken woman.
Complainant–I never get drunk except when you take me out.
The Mayor–Will you give us your promise you will not touch her again.
Defendant–If she will not get drunk.
Complainant–Don't you get drunk yourself?
Defendant–Did I not find you drunk at the George, and thrash you, of which you have the marks about you now.
The Mayor–We can't dismiss the case, as you will not promise not to hit her again. This is the most pitiful case that ever came before the bench. There are faults, no doubt, on both sides, and we take a lenient view of the case, and fine you 5s, and costs.
Defendant–Thank your worships.
August 1, 1866

After being near, cholera finally reached Oswestry:

OUTBREAK OF CHOLERA IN OSWESTRY.–We regret to announce that one fatal case of Asiatic cholera has occurred in this town. On Thursday morning a strong healthy man named Thomas Cadwallader, who kept a small provision and baskets shop in Salop Road, was suddenly taken ill. We believe the disease to be traceable to the fact of a daughter of the deceased, arriving from Liverpool.
September 19, 1866

This is a problem most of the townspeople of Oswestry don't have to face now:

SIR,– I feel constrained to put the public in possession of the particulars respecting the pigsty belonging to this Inn [*the Bell*], which has lately attracted such attention through the complaints of my neighbour, Mr Edward Jones. It is very hard that an inhabitant of the town, after complying at considerable cost with all the requirements of the borough surveyor, should be turned round and told the sty was still a nuisance. I may add that Mr Edward Jones has a sow and pigs now upon his own premises.
I remain, Sir, your obedient servant, MARY ROBERTS.
October 3, 1866

There was one way of solving the bad reputation of a street – change its name:

The Clawdd-du has disappeared in name, and we should be very glad to see it disappear in substance, for it is still the "Black Ditch," though the council had given it the more respectable title of Market-street. On referring to our report of Monday's meeting of the Local Board, it will be seen that the streets have been named, and, to some extent, rearranged; and we hope soon to see the names put up. Cross-street no longer exists, having been merged in Leg-street and Church-street. The New-road has received the appropriate title of Oswald Road, and it is worthy of note that King Oswald's town has not hitherto contained the street of that name.
October 10, 1866

This is a slightly ironic comment:

REJOICINGS IN THE CASTLE FIELDS.–Our correspondent, Mudlark, who dates from the Dismal Swamp, writes to inform us that great rejoicings have taken place in the Castle Fields, in consequence of erection of a street gas lamp in that locality. The lamp is placed at the Calvinistic Methodist Chapel in Albert-street. Our correspondent states that it is proposed to hold a public banquet, and to illuminate the Swamp, in honour of the event, since there can be little doubt that the local board will consider the lamp, which has been provided by the chapel authorities, amply sufficient for all the streets in the New Town, and there will therefore be no more suitable opportunity of publicly rejoicing over the introduction of gas.
October 17, 1866

Here is a warning to parents, to be careful what toys you give your children:

DANGEROUS PLAY.–A few days ago two little boys, aged respectively five and six, were playing together at the top of Willow-street, when one of them struck the other a heavy blow on the head with a hammer. The poor little fellow was seriously injured, but we are glad to understand that he will recover.
October 31, 1866

It's difficult to imagine such a dangerous structure as the Rope Walk bridge, but time and again there were reports such as this one:

On Sunday night, as an old woman named Mrs Cadwallader was passing through the Castle Fields, intending to cross the Rope Walk Bridge, in the dark she walked, instead, through an opening which has been most improbably left by the side of the bridge, and fell into the walk below. She managed to reach home, and a doctor were sent for, and found that, though no bones were broken, she was considerably injured, and is at present, we believe, confined to her bed.
November 7, 1866

FLAVEL'S PATENT COOKING RANGE.
NO PERSON SHOULD BE WITHOUT ONE IN THEIR HOUSE.

FLAVEL'S PATENT KITCHENER.

EDWARD SHAW,

FURNISHING IRONMONGER,

OSWESTRY,

BEGS to inform the public that he has been appointed Agent for the sale of this valuable Kitchener. They are made either with open or close fires ; Roasting, Baking, Stewing, Steaming, and Saucepans kept Boiling on any part of the top plate at the same time ; and last but not least the great Economy in Fuel, as Slack or small Coal will do as well as lumps.

References can be given to parties in the immediate neighbourhood that have the in operation.

E. S., would also direct the attention of parties Furnishing to his new Show Room adjoining his shop, where he has constantly a selection of Bright Berlin, Black Register and Sham Register Grates, Bronzed Fenders, Fire Irons, Toilet Sets, Baths, &c., &c.

£70 was worth about £3000 now:

A WEALTHY DRUNKARD.–Edward Jones, Porthywaen, lime burner, was charged by Sergeant Duncan with being drunk in Leg-street. When taken to the Lock-up £71 9s 8d was found upon him. When he was apprehended there were several suspicious characters about him, and if the police had been a little later he would, doubtless, have been robbed. The Mayor, in fining him 2s 6d and costs, told him he ought to feel much obliged to the police.
January 9, 1867

The Union was the Workhouse at Morda; 4 cwt (hundredweight) is about 200 kilograms, or 450 pounds:

REFUSING TO BREAK STONES.–Thomas Lewis, a tramp, who stated that he came from Bilston, was charged by Mr Fulcher, Master of the Union, with refusing to break 4 cwt of stones, the quantity ordered by the Board of Guardians, in return for his supper and breakfast.–The prisoner, who was a strong young man, said it was quite true that he had refused to break stones, and he would not do so for anybody.–Sentenced to 7 days' imprisonment, with hard labour.
February 6, 1867

Pubs allowed drinkers credit (beer scores), so they could continue to drink after their money had run out. This was strongly criticised:

The Legislature should prohibit actions for the recovery of beer scores. At present many poor fellow, who goes to a public house and there soon loses his senses, is allowed to get drunk on credit, and swallows pint after pint totally unconscious of the debt which is fast accumulating in the publican's books. True, a drunken man cannot incur debt, but such a dictum as that does not avail in the least to protect the tippler against the distortions of those publicans who grow rich on his folly. If ale scores were not recoverable, and every person had to pay before he drank, we may be sure, as the judge says, that the publican would seldomer go to his brewer, and the wife at home would oftener see her husband's money.
February 13, 1867

The turnpike gates were proving increasingly unpopular:

That it is desirable to abolish those obstructions to locomotion, and with them the present expenses system of maintaining the roads, there can be no doubt, though considerable difficulty will perhaps be experience in deciding how the necessary funds shall be raised. The general opinion of those Chambers which have discussed the subject seems to be, that government, having always claimed the free use of turnpike roads for mails and soldiers, ought now to liquidate the existing debts, and abolish all the

turnpike trusts at the same time; and that the mode of raising funds for the future should be settled, by legislation, on a fair and equitable basis.
February 13th 1867

At the beginning of the year there were several complaints about the streets at Town Council meetings:

Mr Bickerton called attention to the state of the Welsh walls, and Mr H Davies also spoke of the way in which the surface of the road had been washed away.
February 13, 1867

The present state of Castle Fields is a disgrace to a civilised community, and it is high time that something should be done. We are only quoting the words of one of the Oswestry town councillors at the last meeting of the Local Board.
March 13, 1867

Mr J Jones asked when Beatrice-street, which had been so often mentioned in that room, was to be put in a proper state of repair. At present it was in the most disgraceful state, and actually dangerous after dark.

Mr D Lloyd wanted to know when Leg-street was to be paved. The surveyor said it would be done when the weather allowed.
March 13, 1867

But the area in most need of repair was certainly Castle Fields, though this correspondent didn't agree with improving it:

Sir,–Nothing could be much worse than the road in the Castle Fields, and the severe comments that have been passed upon it had not been exaggerated, but as bad as it is, I must protest as a ratepayer against the Town Council spending money in making roads for private individuals. If the owners of property choose to build houses in the middle of a field I think it a great injustice that I and others should be called upon to make roads for them, and besides the road leads to nowhere except into these houses.
I am, yours, &c., A Ratepayer
March 27, 1867

A familiar character was back in court:

Richard Jones (*alias* Dick Tycoch) was brought up on remand and charged with stealing a shin of beef, the property of Mr George Jackson, Butcher, Oswestry, on 8 March.
March 20, 1867

One of Oswestry's dignitaries died, the auctioneer who fought off the riots in the Smithfield in 1856:

We regret to recall the death of one of our best-known fellow townsmen, Mr George Hilditch, auctioneer. Twenty years ago, when the question of free trade was agitating the country, Mr Hilditch, then the farmer at Treflach Hall, warmly espoused the cause of Protection. Not long afterwards Mr Hilditch gave up farming and came to live at Oswestry, where he continued his business as an auctioneer. For a few years Mr Hilditch occupied a seat in the Town Council where he did good service by his earnestness on all occasions, and especially by two measures which he was the chief instrument in promoting. One was, the establishment of fortnightly fairs, and the other, the exclusion of itinerant vendors from the Powis Hall, to make room for the dealers in corn. The deceased gentleman, who was in his sixty-seventh year, had only been ill a short time. He expired on Wednesday, at his residence in Roft-street.
April 10, 1867

The mystery of this dead baby seems never to have been solved:

An inquest was held at the King's Head on the body of a male child, which was found dead in the midden [*a privy*] the same morning.
Richard Edwards, labourer, said–I was cleaning out a midden, between four and five o'clock this morning, in the King's Head yard, when I found the body of a child about two feet from the surface of the ground.
Dr Fuller said–I am a surgeon practising in Oswestry. Early this morning Sergeant Duncan brought me the body of a male infant, much decomposed, and in a very filthy condition. I had it washed and found the surface very much decomposed. I opened his chest and made an examination; did not consider it necessary to open the other cavities owing to the advanced state of putrefaction. There was so much decomposition that I did not consider it safe to draw conclusions whether the child being born alive or not. I consider that the child had been born a month. Did not see any marks of violence.
The jury returned a verdict of "Found Dead."
April 10, 1867

This clearly shows the terrible state of some of the roads:

ACCIDENT–On Saturday evening a woman named Elizabeth Vaughan was on her way from Oswestry to the Rookery, Morda, where she lived, when she fell into the gutter, at the turnpike gate. The gutter was flooded by the

rains and if a man (Mr Whitridge's servant) had not been passing at the time, and helped the woman out, she would, most likely, have perished in the water. She was lifted out by the man, however, and taken into the gate-house, whence, after a time, she was removed home in Mr Peate's wag-gon. Inflammation, we believe, set in, and though Mr Wynne, surgeon, attended the woman, and did what medical skill could for her, she died on Monday evening.
April 24, 1867

This railway worker must have been the luckiest in Shropshire:

MIRACULOUS ESCAPE.–On Tuesday (yesterday), as the 9.45 train was leav-ing Gobowen for Oswestry, a goods breaksman [*brakesman*], named Henry Watling, was shunting his train on the down line, when he stepped on to the branch metals. The Oswestry train coming up at the time, he was knocked by one of the buffers of the engine on to the line, with his head across the metals. The engine was driving slowly at the time, and, instead of smashing his head, pushed it gently off the metals, and he lay flat between the metals till the train had passed over him. When he got up it was found that his head was cut but not hurt very much. He was able to go home by the next down train.
May 1, 1867

This article shows some uncanny prescience, because the outbreak of foot and mouth disease started in Oswestry in 1967 – and the same criticism of government incompetence was made then:

THE CATTLE PLAGUE AND THE PLAGUE OF OFFICIAL STUPIDITY.–The history of the recent visitation of this country by the cattle plague will scarcely give the Englishman of 1967 a very exalted idea of the way in which his ancestors were governed. That history, in fact, would consist almost entirely of weak-ness, vacillation, and mistake. First of all the plague was disregarded, then, when negligence had borne its proper fruits, and the effects of the disease were growing too terrible to be disregarded any longer, attempts of the weakest kind, altogether inadequate to the terrible nature of the malady, were made to stay its progress.
May 8, 1867

This is an example of the beer scores mentioned in February; five quarts is ten pints:

FIVE QUARTS A DAY!–Richard Green sued John Plimmer, nailer. Claim, £2 6s 8d, money lent and drink sold. The account contained items of five quarts of drink a day! His Honour said he should not allow such a claim. He should only give judgement for £1 13s, to be paid in weekly instalments of 1s.
May 15, 1867

The police sergeant seems at first to have behaved rather too diligently in this case of a young man getting money from an older woman. He took her money on the promise of marrying her, but then changed his mind – several times:

Sergeant Duncan stated that Ellen Caffery swore Joseph Powell stole £5 18s from her. Powell absconded from Oswestry, and was not apprehended till Saturday night last, when witness found him at Mrs Caffery's house, where he and a number of neighbours were drinking the health of the prisoner and the prosecutrix. Witness disturbed the conviviality of the meeting by telling prisoner that he must go to the lock-up, as there was a warrant against him. Prisoner replied that it was all right, as he had made it up with Mrs Caffery, as she said they were married. The officer, however, was inexorable, and took prisoner to the lock-up, thus making, as Mrs Caffery afterwards said, what she hoped would be the happiest Sunday in her life the most miserable. Sergeant Duncan informed the mayor the prosecutrix now said she gave prisoner the money to buy the wedding clothes with, and it was not true, she stated, that they were married, but they were going to be.

Mrs Caffrey (who is an old woman, while the prisoner is a young man) was next sworn. She said that when she got the warrant she was in a passion, being vexed with him for going away and taking the money but the truth was she gave him the money to buy the wedding clothes with. She handed to the Mayor a letter the prisoner had sent her, commencing "my dear Ellen," and telling her she could put up the banns as soon as she liked, and that he would meet her at the place appointed.

The question here seems to have been: had Joseph Powell got the money from Ellen Caffery honestly? The Mayor tried to find out:

The Mayor: Do you intend to marry this woman?
Prisoner–That is best known to myself.
The Mayor–I think you are a mean fellow to get the money of this old woman on promise of marrying her. What have you done with the money?
Prisoner–I spent it.
The Mayor–Did you think you were doing right when you spent it?
Prisoner–That is best known to myself.
The mayor then reprimanded the man and discharged him; and the police were directed to return to him the money, £1 10s 11d, which was found upon him.
The parties adjourned to the Red Lion, and subsequently to Mrs Caffery's house, to rejoice over the result.
May 22, 1867

After all the expectation of the new waterworks, there were problems, reminiscent of recent complaints about Oswestry water:

Our Oswestry readers will learn with regret, from our report of the local board, that the water from Penygwelly will always be discoloured, except

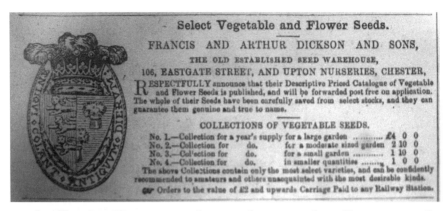

after filtration. We recommend our readers to purchase filters at once, for the Penygwelly water is much more wholesome for drinking purposes than any which they can obtain from local springs. Discolouration of the water, it is said, arises from the peat, and causes no unpleasant taste.
June 5, 1867

The Advertiser continued to campaign for better streets:

We hear that Oswald Road is to be put in proper order next autumn. The present time, it is said, is unfavourable to road-making, and we can only hope, therefore, that the summer will not be a very wet one, and that when autumn comes we shall not be again disappointed. Meanwhile, why does not some patriotic Oswestrian, of sufficient standing to make his fall noticeable, break his leg in Castle-street, and bring the question of putting it in decent order to a practical issue.
June 5, 1867

The excuse in this case seems to be somewhat unlikely:

ASSAULT.–Charlotte Rowlands was charged with assaulting Mrs Titley, on 13 May. Mrs Titley stated that she was going down street, when defendant threw a pail of dirty water over her, and said, "Take that, you d— old bitch." Defendant admitted throwing the water over complainant, but stated that it was accidentally done.–Fined 4s 6d, and 15s costs.
June 5, 1867

Children are presumably meant by 'rascals':

DISGRACEFUL OUTRAGES.–On Saturday night some rascals visited the gardens at Llwyn Terrace, Bridge Terrace, and other places in town, and stole the best flowers they could find. The police have shrewd suspicions as to the direction in which enquiries should be made, and we hope the rascals will be found out.
June 26, 1867

This shows Shropshire to be leading the country in an unfortunate way:

Shropshire, we find, is far ahead of any other county in the drunken returns. The number of public and beer houses, on the other hand, is below the average, and not much more than half as high as in Cambridgeshire, where the drunkenness is only one fourth of the average!
July 3, 1867

This is the first of several tales of children let loose into the countryside at ages that seem very young to us. It's about two miles from Babbins Wood to the Queen's Head or to Oswestry:

A LITTLE WANDERER.–A few evenings ago a little child, six years old, was sent from Babbins Wood to the Queen's Head to buy treacle. On its return home the child lost its way, and, wandering to Oswestry, found its way down the Llys Lane, and into an adjoining field, where it lay down and fell asleep. Meanwhile, of course, great was the dismay at home, and search was made in every direction, but not till morning was the child discovered, lying asleep in the field, with a jar of treacle by its side.
August 28, 1867

There must have been some notoriety about this couple, to have been 'followed through the street by a crowd of people':

AN ELOPEMENT.–On Monday evening, a young man and a young lady, who had arrived in this town that day, attended the Christy Minstrels' entertainment at the public hall. In the course of the day, too, a policeman arrived to look after the young lady, who was the daughter of a Shropshire clergyman, and who had eloped with a carpenter's apprentice. At the door of the hall the young lady was met by the policeman, and she was followed by him, and a crowd of people, to the house where she had taken up her abode. The policeman endeavoured to persuade her to return home, but in vain. She asserts that, being of age, she shall please herself, and she and her fortunate adorer, who are lodging at different houses, spent yesterday together in Oswestry, where, in due time, we suppose, they intend to get married. The course of their love has run far from smooth. Some time ago, we believe, the young lady was sent from home to take up her residence in another part of the county, with a policeman's wife, who had served as a nurse in the family. From the policeman's house she escaped to Oswestry, and arrived here on Monday, as we have stated. The course which has been pursued in this case, we must say, does not appear to us very well calculated to effect the object which the young lady's father has in view. The policeman, at any rate, might have spared her the annoyance of being followed through the street by a crowd of people.
September 11, 1867

At this time the Cottage Hospital was at Herbert Villas in Castle Street:

We observe with great satisfaction that Mr Parry and Mr Jacks have undertaken the paving of Castle-street from the Cottage Hospital to the termination of their property, and a number of men have been busily employed in rescuing the street from the disgraceful condition in which it has so long remained. Let us hope the other proprietors in Castle-street will awake to their duty, and follow Mr Parry's example.
October 2, 1867

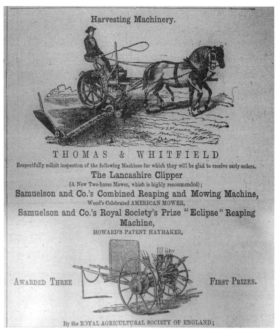

Harvesting Machinery.

THOMAS & WHITFIELD

Respectfully solicit inspection of the following Machines for which they will be glad to receive early orders.

The Lancashire Clipper
(A New Two-horse Mower, which is highly recommended);

Samuelson and Co.'s Combined Reaping and Mowing Machine,
Wood's Celebrated AMERICAN MOWER,

Samuelson and Co.'s Royal Society's Prize "Eclipse" Reaping Machine,
HOWARD'S PATENT HAYMAKER,

AWARDED THREE   FIRST PRIZES.

By the ROYAL AGRICULTURAL SOCIETY OF ENGLAND;

For some time there had been moves for a new Cottage Hospital:

The subscribers to the Oswestry Cottage Hospital will soon be called together, we suppose, to decide upon the site of the new building, which so large a sum has already been raised. Is it too much to hope that rivalries of recent date will be magnanimously forgotten, and that what a correspondent last week called "the splendid but comparatively useless" Victoria Rooms will be devoted to the excellent purpose of an hospital?
November 6, 1867

This story demonstrates the enormous contrast between a drunken Oswestry Saturday night in 1867 ...and a delightfully sober one now:

The cases of Drunkenness heard at the Oswestry Petty Session on Friday called forth a remark from one of the magistrates which the police will do well to remember. The scenes witnessed in Oswestry on Saturday night are exceedingly disgraceful, especially to some of the publicans. The streets are full of drunken men and women, and in Willow-street, for instance, the respectable inhabitants are constantly disturbed by quarrels whose origin is in the public house.
November 6, 1867

Thomas Jones, the fireman at this coal mine near Morda, must have been the unluckiest man in Shropshire:

EXTRAORDINARY FATAL ACCIDENT AT COAL PIT.–On Monday afternoon an inquest was opened at the Drill Inn, near Oswestry, on the body of Thomas Jones, a fireman at the Old British Coal Pit, who had been killed in an accident of a very remarkable character. It is necessary to explain that the only persons now employed at the Old Pit are two men and a boy (fourteen years old), who are engaged in attending to machinery for pumping out water, in anticipation of an eventual communication with the neighbouring New British Pit. For the pumping an iron barrel, weighing about half a ton, is employed, and this barrel, when brought to the surface (about 330 feet from the water), is shipped on the truck, where it empties itself. The duty of the boy was to move this truck backwards and forwards as the barrel descended and ascended the pit, and the two men were employed, one as engine driver and the deceased as fireman. On Sunday morning, when the accident happened, the driver and the boy took a short rest in the engine house, about six o'clock, whilst the fireman got up the steam, which had gone so low that the barrel was left at the top of the pit, instead of the bottom, where it is usually left at such intervals; and, unfortunately, they both fell asleep.

They were woken up, some time later, by the steam whistling. The boy ran outside to see to the truck, and gave the driver the signal for working the engine, so that the barrel could be lifted from the truck and then lowered into the pit.

The driver, however, just awakened from sleep, seems to have imagined that the barrel was at the bottom as usual, and, without examining the indicator, which would have showed him where it was, or looking outside, where he might have seen it by means of a lamp placed there for the purpose, he worked the engine to bring the barrel to the surface. The consequence was, that the barrel was carried to the top of the pulley, about fifty feet high, and, rebounding, flew over the engine house, and alighted the other side, some seventy feet from the mouth of the pit. Search was immediately made for the fireman, who was not in the engine house when the accident occurred, and a considerable time elapsed before he was found. His dead body was then discovered partially beneath the barrel which had fallen upon him just as he happened to be standing outside the house, attending to the donkey engine that supplies the boiler with water.

The OSWESTRY ADVERTISER,
Montgomeryshire Mercury, North Shropshire Gazette, and Local Journal for the Borders of Wales.

The barrel, of all the places it could have gone, landed on top of the fireman, killing him immediately:

The barrel had struck his head and was resting on his chest, and steam was issuing from the pipes. Had the rope to which the barrel was attached been a yard longer or shorter, or had the barrel fallen, by an inch or two, in a different place, the poor fellow would have escaped. The barrel, in its fall, did no damage to the machinery beyond breaking some of the steam pipes, but the rope, a very strong iron one, fell through the roof of the engine house, carrying in a large portion of it; and the driver, and a boy who was sleeping in the building, narrowly escaped death.

The jury returned a verdict of "Accidental Death." The deceased man, who was thirty-five years old, leaves a wife and three children.

January 8, 1868

This report laments that, if a stranger should leave the train at Oswestry Railway Station, this would be his experience as 'he trudged and splashed his weary, dirty way along the Oswald Road':

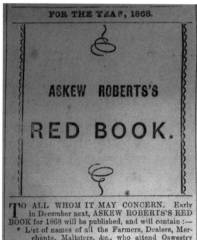

In 1868 John Askew Roberts sold the Oswestry Advertiser to Edward Woodall, but he continued to write several books on the area, including his RED BOOK.

That road, at the present moment, is more literally a river of mud than any other road we ever saw; and it is simply impossible to walk along it without suffering an amount of discomfort which no one ought to be compelled to endure in a civilised town. The view from the railways stations gives such a dirty, and desolate idea of Oswestry to the visitor, that we cannot wonder at the uncomplimentary remarks too often made about the town which ought to be one of the most delightful places of residence in the Kingdom. A miserable waste of mud stretching away towards Leg-street, broken here and there by little hillocks of stone and rubbish and skirted on one side by an uneven, ill conditioned heap of dirt and ashes called a footpath.

January 15, 1868

Or, as a letter writer puts it more satirically:

SIR,–Your readers will be glad to hear that Hercules is cleansing the Augean stables–at least, one old man has been put to scrape Oswald Road.

Yours, DIRTYBOOTS.

January 22, 1868

This next report happened at a time when the Fenians, forerunners of the IRA, were still campaigning. The Old Bank was in Willow Street, near the Cross:

A STUPID TRICK.–On Thursday night some stupid fellow threw a quantity of explosive material–nitro-glycerine we understand–about the streets, and caused no little annoyance to some people, though he did not succeed in inducing anyone to believe that "the Fenians had done it." The largest quantity was placed near the Old Bank, but it was also scattered up Church-street, and the slightest concussion, even the blowing of the wind, caused it to explode, and to disturb the sleep of the neighbouring inhabitants.

FLAVEL & Co's PRIZE KITCHENER

THOMAS AND WHITFIELD
Solicit inspection of their Extensive Stock of KITCHEN RANGES, REGISTER STOVE GRATES, DINING and DRAWING ROOM FENDERS and FIRE IRONS, SPARK GUARDS, COAL VASES, BATHS and TOILETTE WARE.
BRADFORD'S WASHING and MANGLING MACHINES.
Agents for WHEELER and WILSON'S Celebrated SEWING MACHINES.
THE CROSS, OSWESTRY.

January 29, 1868

This is a report on the great storms and floods of February, 1868:

The rivers, which rose with almost unprecedented rapidity and to an almost unequalled height, carried away large numbers of sheep, sapped the foundations of bridges, and injured railways, involving in one case a fatal accident on the Cambrian line, and in other ways issued in destruction and death. The storm of wind, which was the fiercest that has ever been known in the district, except perhaps by some of the oldest inhabitants, of course increased greatly the disastrous effects of the flood, which looked like a stormy sea. At Oswestry, for instance, the roofs of several houses were seriously damaged, many yards of wooden palisades were blown down in Oswald Road, one of the lofty poplar trees at Bickerton's Pool [*on Beatrice Street, near where King Street is now*] snapped about four feet from the ground, and another tree, which fell on the Welsh Walls, knocked away part of the wall on each side of the road. Other trees blew down in various parts of the town, and many in the country round, in Porkington Park, Aston Park, and, in fact, in all directions.

February 5, 1868

If only there had been cameras in 1868:

A Novel Sale in the Smithfield.–An old man named William Newnes, a drover of Harmer Hill, was charged by Sergeant Duncan with being drunk and incapable in the Smithfield on Wednesday afternoon. The prisoner was found drunk and lying in a pig pen with a crowd of youngsters round him. His legs had been tied to the bars of the pen and one of the juveniles was trying to dispose of him by public auction. Prisoner knew nothing at all about the matter and his character being hitherto spotless, as far as the police books were concerned, he was discharged with a caution.
March 4, 1868

Typhoid is much less dangerous than cholera, but was still very serious:

The Health of Oswestry.–If it be true that people are dying in unusual numbers from Typhoid Fever, it can be but small consolation to know that "in other towns the rate of mortality is high." No one with a nose on his face can for a moment doubt that the Town Council of Oswestry have not hitherto sufficiently empowered their surveyor to deal with nuisances. There is scarcely a street in the town in which vile and filthy slops are not thrown from the door–why are not the offenders fined? There are pig-sties in close quarters; smelling slaughter-houses, and imperfect drains in every direction–although £20,000 has been spent in purifying measures. Local Board-men talk, and editors write, and the inhabitants pay heavy taxes; and no improvement results.
April 8, 1868

Continuing from the above report:

Mortality in Oswestry.–From the Registrar-General's return of deaths for the quarter ending March 31st, we learn that–"The deaths in the town and parish of Oswestry during the last quarter were much above the average. In the town, for the last eight years, the average was 35, and in the parish 30; whereas the deaths in the last quarter were, in the town 47, and in the parish 42, and this in the town of Oswestry with a decreasing population, it being estimated that the population of the town is less by nearly 500 than it was two years ago. Measles, scarletina, and

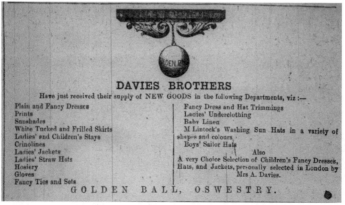

DAVIES BROTHERS

Have just received their supply of NEW GOODS in the following Departments, viz :—

Plain and Fancy Dresses	Fancy Dress and Hat Trimmings
Prints	Ladies' Underclothing
Sunshades	Baby Linen
White Tucked and Frilled Skirts	M'Lintock's Washing Sun Hats in a variety of
Ladies' and Children's Stays	shapes and colours
Crinolines	Boys' Sailor Hats
Ladies' Jackets	Also
Ladies' Straw Hats	A very Choice Selection of Children's Fancy Dresses,
Hosiery	Hats, and Jackets, personally selected in London by
Gloves	Mrs A. Davies.
Fancy Ties and Sets	

GOLDEN BALL, OSWESTRY.

typhoid fever have been and still continue very prevalent amongst children in the town of Oswestry."
May 13, 1868

Despite that, this was remarked on, even if these days it might not seem so extraordinary:

LONGEVITY.–There are a brother and two sisters resident in Oswestry and the immediate neighbourhood whose ages average eighty-six, one of them being eighty-four, the second eighty-six, and the other eighty-eight.
July 22, 1868

After all the efforts to improve the Castle Bank, this happened:

Yesterday morning, about 11 o'clock, it was discovered that the Castle Bank was on fire! The dry grass on the side sloping down to the Powis Market was burning, and some of the small trees had ignited. Meanwhile, however, a number of persons had collected on the hill, and almost succeeded in stamping out the fire. The water was soon brought to play upon the spot, and in a short time a black patch on the hillside was all the sign that remained of the mimic conflagration. It is not unlikely that children who were playing on the hill caused the mischief.
July 29, 1868

A list of the deaths in Oswestry, labelled under 'Zymotic diseases', which is an old term for acute infectious illnesses:

UNDER FOURTEEN YEARS		ADULTS	
Scarlet fever	14	Typhoid Fever	2
Measles	2	Diarrhoea	1
Diarrhoea	3	Cancer	1
Hooping cough	1	Diseases of Liver and Kidneys	3
Acute diseases of chest	4	Tubercular Disease of Chest	5
Debility from birth	5	Chronic Ulcer and Gangrene	1
Tubercular Diseases of Bowels	6	Natural Death (Inquest)	1
Sunstroke	1	Softening of the Brain	1
Natural Death (Inquest)	1	Dropsy	1
Convulsions	4	Disease of Heart and Larynx	1
		Erysipelas of Leg	1
		Senile Decay	2
		Pneumonia	2
Total	41	Total	22

October 7, 1868

After all the money spent on the waterworks, they didn't seem to work very well:

Mr George Owen said–Mr Mayor and gentlemen,–I beg to call your attention to a matter of the greatest importance to the town of Oswestry. I mean the insufficiency of the supply of water to our town, which must arise from

one of three causes, a too limited watershed, bad management, or leakage or defects in the pipes or works. As to the first of these causes, I visited Penygwelly, and I have no hesitation in saying that with proper management sufficient water could be collected to supply Oswestry, were it double the size. (Hear, hear.) What I should propose doing would be to erect a dam across the stream above the weir, and a reservoir may be formed there capable of holding millions of gallons. Without something of this sort is done, you may depend upon it we shall be in the same fix next summer.
October 7, 1868

This was the last enlargement of the Advertiser, and this time only very slightly:

ENLARGEMENT OF THE ADVERTISER.–The Proprietors have the pleasure of announcing that on Wednesday, January 6 next, the Advertiser sheet will be enlarged to *Times*-size, and printed in entirely new type.
November 25, 1868

There was a general election, when the Liberals under Gladstone won, and considerable upheaval during canvassing:

Who can wish for annual parliaments after the experience of the last fortnight? In our own district, happily, there are no lists of "dead and wounded" to add to the records of the fight, as there are in some places; but even here, if there are no broken heads, there are broken promises, which are worse; and if there has been no physical violence, there has been violence of another and more deplorable kind. The commotion of an election throws to the surface an amount of tyranny and trickery on the one hand, and weakness and cowardice on the other.
December 2, 1868

There is a pleasing sprit of generosity in this report:

A GYPSY ENCAMPMENT.–A site of this kind, which is seldom witnessed in the neighbourhood of Oswestry, may now be seen in a field nearly opposite the Cambrian station, where quite a host of gypsies have pitched their tents, which are many in number and of various shapes and different dimensions. The camp is said to be honoured with the presence of the king and queen of the gypsy tribe, with whom, we believe, an interview may be obtained on the payment of a small admission fee. During their stay here, the gypsies intend giving a series of public balls, and for that purpose have engaged one of the best bands in the district.
December 2, 1868

Another story of a wandering child; it is about six miles from Oswestry to Chirk:

STRAYING FAR FROM HOME.–On Sunday morning a girl, about seven years old, living at Weston, came to town, against her mother's wish, to see the mayor's procession, and attended church with his worship. After service the little thing took the wrong direction, and, instead of finding her way

to Weston, wandered off towards Chirk. The mother naturally became alarmed, and search was made to the missing child, who could not be found that day. The next morning, however, a letter was received from a cottage the other side of Chirk, stating that the child was there, and she was, of course, at once fetched home.
December 16, 1868

This illustrates again the danger of trying to get to Castle Fields:

A NARROW ESCAPE.–On Saturday last a little girl very narrowly escaped drowning, on the rope walk. The grating at the mouth of the sewer on the walk being choked up with debris, a considerable quantity of surface water accumulated owing to the heavy rains, and after the obstruction had been removed, of course the water rushed down the sewer very rapidly. While this was going on, a little girl fell into the stream, which was carrying her towards the sewer, when she was observed by William Thomas, the man in charge of the walk, who seized her hand, just in the nick of time, and so saved from what otherwise must have been certain death.
December 30, 1868

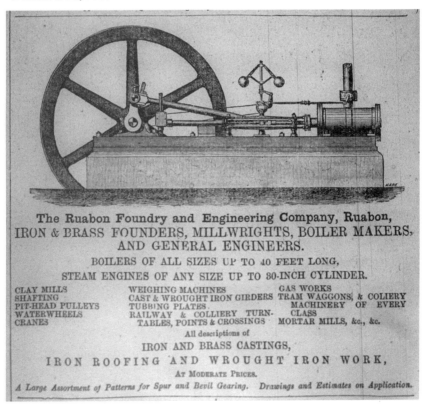

The Ruabon Foundry and Engineering Company, Ruabon,
IRON & BRASS FOUNDERS, MILLWRIGHTS, BOILER MAKERS,
AND GENERAL ENGINEERS.
BOILERS OF ALL SIZES UP TO 40 FEET LONG,
STEAM ENGINES OF ANY SIZE UP TO 30-INCH CYLINDER.

CLAY MILLS
SHAFTING
PIT-HEAD PULLEYS
WATERWHEELS
CRANES

WEIGHING MACHINES
CAST & WROUGHT IRON GIRDERS
TUBBING PLATES
RAILWAY & COLLIERY TURN-
TABLES, POINTS & CROSSINGS

GAS WORKS
TRAM WAGGONS, & COLLIERY
MACHINERY OF EVERY
CLASS
MORTAR MILLS, &c., &c.

All descriptions of
IRON AND BRASS CASTINGS,
IRON ROOFING AND WROUGHT IRON WORK,
AT MODERATE PRICES.
A Large Assortment of Patterns for Spur and Bevil Gearing. Drawings and Estimates on Application.

This is the third, and probably most extraordinary, story of a wandering child; Oswestry to Leamington is 90 miles:

A LOST CHILD.–A little fellow nine years of age, named Alfred Redfern (of Leamington), on a visit to his grandmother, Mrs Parry, Dispensary, left the house on Monday morning week, ostensibly for the purpose of proceeding to the National School. Night came on, and the boy not having returned to his grandmother's, considerable anxiety was felt, and when the morning of Tuesday still found him absent, the anxiety of course increased. Ultimately the police were communicated with. Nothing, however, was definitely ascertained as to his whereabouts until yesterday, when his grandmother received intelligence that he had arrived at home, having walked, and, by "hook or crook" sustained himself the whole of the way, and what is more–though only a delicate boy–he arrived at home "looking well."
March 10, 1869

This shows that little progress had been made on the subject of the Castle Bank:

Seventeen years ago, in January, 1852, we called attention to the disgraceful state of the Castle Bank, and advocated its conversion into what we called a "central and attractive pleasure ground." The Castle Bank ought to be public property, and only as public property will it be properly attended to. With an outlay which would make no material difference in the rates, it might be converted into an ornament to the town and a pleasant resort, where many would go for the sake of the charming view to be obtained from the summit.
April 28, 1869

The French prisoners mentioned here helped to re-lay the grass of the Racecourse:

THE FRENCH PRISONERS' TOMBSTONES.–As our readers know, some of the French prisoners at the time of Napoleon's wars were on parole in Oswestry, and in the Old Church-yard their tombs may be seen to this day, but in a dilapidated state. An effort has been started to restore them, and the officers of the Yeomanry were asked to contribute to the fund, which we hope will be successful.
May 26, 1869

Another problem marriage, but where for once drink was not the cause of the problems:

A MARRIAGE NOT MADE IN HEAVEN.–John Cheesman, engine driver, Gatestreet, was charged with assaulting his wife, Martha Cheesman.–Complainant said that while she was sitting at the breakfast table with her two little boys, her husband was walking up and down the house, talking to himself and "imagining things that was not so." She kept still until he had

done and she then said, "Oh, you've been to that there Bridge-terrace, I suppose." That was all that passed before he gave her a blow, knocking both her and the chair she was sitting in down. She then said, "You think I have no witness; but thank God I've the boys." He made no reply, but went out, and she went for a summons.

The magistrate asked Mrs Cheesman what she meant by asking him if he had been to Bridge Terrace. She replied:

His brothers live there, and he was saying just the words I had heard them say to him, about looking like an unhappy man.–Mr Croxon: What were the words he said that offended you?–Complainant: He said I did not care anything for him, and the children did not care anything for him; that I was ruining the children and they were treating him like a dog.–Mr Croxon: is this the first time he struck you?–Complainant: No; he has done it often, and I have been all over black places, from my head to my heels.–Defendant: From natural causes.–Complainant: I do not mind what he says, or any bad language, he is only heaping coals on his own head; but I cannot stand the blows, and there must be some alterations in them. Nothing will hurt me but the blows, for I can stand anything he can say.–Mr Croxon: Had he had any beer that morning?–Complainant: No; he's a sober man. He does not get beer.–Mr Croxon: How long have you been married?–Complainant: Since '43.–Defendant: Twenty-six years.

Mr Cheesman claimed he hadn't hit his wife. He said he only pushed her with his flat hand:

Complainant, in reply to a question, said her husband generally gave her all his money, though he kept a sovereign now and then.–Defendant said she had all his money–two guineas a week–and she would neither make his

shirts nor do any mending for him.–Mr Croxon: Why don't you put some of your money in the Savings Bank? Defendant: It goes into the sinking fund, instead of the Savings Bank. (A laugh.)–Mr Croxon: You had better put half your wages in the Savings Bank.–Defendant went on to say that his wife was the most contrary woman in the town, and she sat with her back to him at the table and turned the children against him. Complainant (interrupting): There–let me speak.–Mr Croxon: You be quiet, or you'll have to be bound over.–Complainant: I do not care about being bound over. I have been bound over twenty-five years now. (Laughter.)–The Mayor said it was pitiable to see two persons who had lived together so long at the court under such circumstances. There were many redeeming points in defendant's character, and the magistrates thought the ends of justice would be met by his paying the costs.–Defendant: But I must have these blows arranged. (A laugh.)–Mr Lloyd advised the parties to go home and try to live peaceably together; they however, left the court in anything but a friendly spirit, complainant having reluctantly paid the expenses because her husband was destitute of money.
June 2, 1869

This animal is considerably friskier than the wild cow of 1863:

ADVENTURES WITH A BULL.–
On Wednesday morning Mr Evans of Sweeney, wishing to send a bull to the fair, gave it in charge to a man named John Lewis. Mr Evans led the animal out of the yard quietly enough, but on the road it turned upon Lewis, threw him into the air, and trampled upon him when he fell. The poor fellow had his arm fractured, and was removed to the Cottage Hospital, where he is going on as well as can be expected. Mr Evans got hold of the bull, which

AT
·O S W E S T R Y,
ON
FRIDAY and SATURDAY, MAY 7TH AND 8TH.
A OR THE
"*FAMED WANDERING TEACHER OF NATURAL HISTORY.*"
M A N D E R S'
GRAND NATIONAL STAR MENAGERIE
Will Enter the Town about Noon, in
BRILLIANT PROCESSION,
Headed by the Great
AFRICAN LION-TAMER, MACCOMO,
IN HIS
SUPERB GOLDEN BAND CHARIOT
Drawn by Elephants, Camels and Dromedaries;
THE GRAND DRAGON CARRIAGE,
Drawn by the Great African Elephant, Brahmin Bulls,
and four richly-caparisoned Piebald Mules—*the Gold alone*
on these State Carriages cost Several Hundred Pounds; the
MAGNIFICENT HARNESS WAGGON, drawn by an
Elephant and Dromedaries; the GREAT MANDER-
NETHECA, drawn by Twelve Splendid Greys, with Silver
Trappings; followed by
FIFTEEN IMMENSE CARAVANS,
DRAWN BY
SIXTY POWERFUL DRAUGHT HORSES!
"These fine cattle are a *sight* in themselves."

went quietly with him for some distance, when another man volunteered to take it. The bull then, however, became savage again, broke away, and as the man was getting onto a wall, helped him in an unpleasant manner in the ascent. The man remained on the wall, we believe, for an hour and a half! Eventually Mr Evans had the beast taken back to the farm.
June 9, 1869

This refers to the long footbridge that still stands over the railway track at Gobowen Road:

Our readers will be pleased to see that at last there is a prospect of having a footbridge created over the Cambrian and Great Western Railways, from Beatrice-street to the Shelf Bank. At present the lines have to be crossed in very dangerous fashion, and the wonder is that accidents have not often occurred.
July 7, 1869

More drinking on a Saturday night (5s was worth about £10 now):

A NEW EGG TRICK.–Richard Thomas, of Osbaston, was brought up charged with being drunk in the Cross Market, on Saturday night.–Sergeant Duncan said he found defendant intoxicated, and was told that he had been standing on his head in a hamper of eggs belonging to Mrs Lewis, of the Clawddu. He (the officer) saw the eggs, which were 300 in number, but there appeared to be about half of them broken. A fine of 5s was imposed, with 5s 6d costs.
July 21, 1869

This fire was probably the most destructive in the town for these years, despite the new waterworks being in operation:

A DISASTROUS FIRE.–Early on Sunday morning the cry of "Fire," happily so strange to the ears of the people of this town, was heard in the streets, and a large number of the inhabitants were soon hurrying in the direction of the flames. The scene of the conflagration was the premises occupied by Mr John Jones, skinner, at the top of Willow-street, and when, at two o'clock, the first half-dozen spectators had arrived, they saw a great mass of flames shooting up into the air, which, happily, was perfectly still. The flames had been discovered a short time before by a woman living close by.

Unfortunately, the person in charge of turning the water on, the turncock, couldn't be found, his address being described as "somewhere in Castle Fields":

Time was lost in finding that necessary official, whose address surely ought to be prominently announced, and additional time in his expedition up the Racecourse-road to the spot where the water had to be turned on, so that it must have been nearly 3 o'clock before any water could be brought to play upon the fire.

Meanwhile, of course, the work of destruction had been going on fiercely, and the roof of the building had fallen in. The cries of pigs, too, roasting in the flames, were audible, and it was quite impossible to save the poor animals from their fate–except in one case, in which a man named Simon Roberts rushed to the rescue of an animal of his own, and pulled it out just in time to save himself from being crushed by the falling roof. The interval between the arrival of the first spectators and the time when the water was turned on was occupied by many of them in carrying skins and other things from the premises, and thus much valuable property was saved.

When the water was finally turned on, though, there were still problems:

When, however, the pipes had been provided with water it was discovered that they leaked badly, and skins had to be employed in preventing the leakage. For an hour the water was struggling with the fire for mastery, and when, about four o'clock, the flames died out, it was for want of further fuel to feed on, for Mr Jones's building was completely gutted, and its contents were destroyed. Some of the animals that were in danger escaped, and ran down Willow-street; and one of them, it is stated, committed involuntary suicide by rushing back into the flames, where it perished.
August 25, 1869

The cattle plague had been virtually eradicated, but another lesser disease, more familiar to us, arrived:

The outbreak of the foot and mouth disease came before the Board, and was afterwards discussed by the county magistrates. From our report of their meeting, it will be seen that disease has spread extensively amongst the cattle in the district.
September 8, 1869

Mrs Ormsby Gore was the mother of the local MP, and widow of William Ormsby Gore, who had died in 1863:

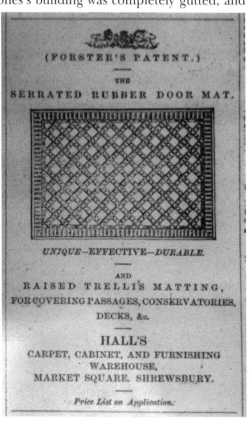

(FORSTER'S PATENT.)

THE

SERRATED RUBBER DOOR MAT.

UNIQUE—EFFECTIVE—DURABLE.

AND

RAISED TRELLIS MATTING,

FOR COVERING PASSAGES, CONSERVATORIES,

DECKS, &c.

HALL'S

CARPET, CABINET, AND FURNISHING

WAREHOUSE,

MARKET SQUARE, SHREWSBURY.

Price List on Application.

It is with much regret that we have to record today the death of Mrs Ormsby Gore, of Porkington, a lady whose name will be familiar to most of our readers in Shropshire and North Wales. Mrs Gore had attained such a good old age, that her death will hardly excite surprise, although her illness was sudden and of short duration. She was in her eighty-eighth year at the time of her death.
September 15, 1869

This man was charged with an unusual offence – not wearing a hat:

DRUNKENNESS.–At the Police Court yesterday, John Jones of Pant, shoemaker, was charged before the Mayor with being drunk and going about the streets bare-headed, at half past three in the morning.
September 29, 1869

This cow seems more placid than others reported:

THE OLD WOMAN AND HER COW.–Last week a cow belonging to Richard Martin was stolen out of a field near Plasmadoc. P.C.Morris, accompanied by Mrs Martin, traced the cow to Oswestry. As soon as Mrs Martin saw the cow, the good old dame exclaimed, "Cherry, Cherry, what made you leave me?" threw her arms around the cow's neck, and kissed it–the latest illustration of the old saying that "there is no accounting for taste."
September 29, 1869

The sewerage system and the waterworks seemed to have improved the health of Oswestry; the population of Oswestry was about 4000 in 1869:

The remarkable improvement in the sanitary condition of Oswestry, as compared with last year, by directing attention to the subject has brought into prominence a very satisfactory fact. The deaths for the quarter ending September, 1869, only amounted to twenty-one, a figure unprecedentedly low in the returns of several years past. Going back as far as 1862, we find that the nearest approach to the return of the past quarter was in 1865, when the number of deaths was twenty-four; and the population at that time was smaller than it is at present.
October 13, 1869

At last, too, Oswestry would have a new hospital:

The ceremony of laying the foundation-stone of the Oswestry and Ellesmere Cottage Hospital was very successfully performed on Monday. The town kept holiday, every shop being closed from noon in honour of the event; and all the inhabitants turned out to see the long procession which accompanied Sir Watkin Williams Wynn and his brother freemasons, and the Mayor and Corporation, from the Guildhall to the new building on the Welsh Walls. There the Masonic ritual was duly carried out, a few short speeches were made, and the stone was laid.
November 3, 1869

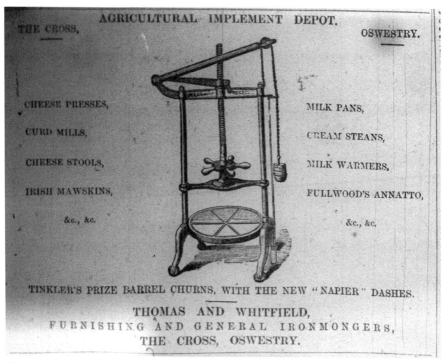

THE CROSS,　　AGRICULTURAL IMPLEMENT DEPOT.　　OSWESTRY.

CHEESE PRESSES,

CURD MILLS,

CHEESE STOOLS,

IRISH MAWSKINS,

&c., &c.

MILK PANS,

CREAM STEANS,

MILK WARMERS,

FULLWOOD'S ANNATTO,

&c., &c.

TINKLER'S PRIZE BARREL CHURNS, WITH THE NEW "NAPIER" DASHES.

THOMAS AND WHITFIELD,
FURNISHING AND GENERAL IRONMONGERS,
THE CROSS, OSWESTRY.

They started young in those days:

A NARROW ESCAPE FROM DEATH.–John Williams, a boy twelve years old, was charged with being drunk and incapable of taking care of himself, in the horse market, on Wednesday afternoon. The lad is in service at Bwlchyci-bau, 3 miles from Llansaintffraid; and on Wednesday he came to Oswestry with his mistress, Mrs Howell, who imprudently gave him some ale. The effect of the ale upon the lad was that he became insensible and quite black in the face. His mistress put him into a wagon and covered him with some straw. Fortunately, some bystanders observed the lad's condition and called the attention of P.S.Duncan to him. The sergeant conveyed the lad to the police station, where Dr Beresford applied remedial measures and consciousness was restored. When asked what he had been drinking, he replied, "Only a quart." It was Dr Beresford's opinion that unless the lad had had medical attention he would unquestionably have died.–The Mayor discharged the defendant with a caution against being led into so dangerous a predicament in the future.
November 10, 1869

While the sewer system was finished, and at last Oswestry was no longer 'the town of many smells', everything was still not right:

DISGRACEFUL DRAINAGE.–MR BICKERTON wished to know if there was any pos-
sibility of the Corporation obtaining any recompense for the work now
being done in the Cross. It had been found all the way down the street,
that drain pipes had been laid as much as 9½ inches the wrong way in the
drain. (Cries of "Shame!") And Mr Smith had no idea when he was going
to finish the work of repair.–The MAYOR: The drain pipes must have sunk.–
MR BICKERTON said they could not sink, and when the manhole was come
to he was afraid it would be found 18 inches out.–The TOWN CLERK, reply-
ing to the question, said that the corporation might apply for recompense;
but as the contractor, Mr Bugbird, had got a certificate, he was afraid they
would not succeed.
November 10, 1869

In the years of this book, the Advertizer reports many deaths of children in accidents, usually by being burnt when their clothes caught fire. This is another terrible
accident:

DREADFUL DEATH OF A CHILD.–On Monday evening the borough coroner
held an inquest, respecting the death of Sara Evans, two years old, the
daughter of Edward Evans, labourer.–Mrs Evans said: I am the wife of
Edward Evans, a labourer. The deceased was my child, and was two years
old on 26th of September last. I was in bed on Saturday afternoon, and
I dosed asleep, as near as I can tell, about five o'clock, or perhaps a little
after. The child came upstairs while the kettle was on the fire, and I was
not aware of it. She must have drunk from the kettle, or got the steam into
her mouth; she screamed out, "Oh my mouth!" I took and dressed her
mouth with butter first, and then I sent my little girl for some honey, and
dressed it again with that.

These were not probably the most effective treatments. The mother called in a
neighbour, and a doctor was sent for, but too late:

She fell asleep for a while–slept not more than an hour and a half, and
then awoke and seemed to be in great pain; so I called Mrs Hughes in. Mrs
Hughes took the child off my knee, and told me that she did not live many
minutes; I did not exactly see her die. The child was not in a burial club.
Mrs Mary Hughes, widow, said: The child did not appear to be in any pain
at all; it never stirred. There was a blister on the lower lip; I could not
see anything on the mouth. I had seen the child about four o'clock that
afternoon, when she came into my house, quite well, laughing and playing. The father came for me; I sent him for a doctor, and he went on to
Mr Davies's house.–The Coroner explained that in such cases of scalding,
the top of the windpipe swells tremendously, as in croup, and causes suf-
focation by preventing air from getting into the lungs.–The jury returned
a verdict of "Accidental Death."
November 17, 1869

Gas lighting was useful, but also dangerous, especially when there were candles around. The gas works in Oswestry was next to the cemetery, where JT Hughes is now. We are not told what happened to the servant girl in this report:

GAS EXPLOSION.–On Friday morning last an explosion of a serious character occurred at Victoria House, Willow-street. Our readers are aware that very considerable excavations in connection with the town drainage are being carried out in the vicinity of the Cross. During the progress of the works, that portion of the street opposite Victoria House, was opened up; and it is supposed that the gas mains were injured, and an escape of gas ensued. On the morning in question, about nine o'clock, Mr Davies's servant girl took a lighted candle into the cellar, and instantaneously an explosion followed. So great was the shock, that the counter was loosened from its fixings, and thrown to the opposite side of the shop; the flooring of the shop was split up, the quantity of goods burnt in the cellar, and some muffs and other stock singed in the shop window.
December 1, 1869

This is a particularly horrible industrial accident that happened to young John Edwards:

FATAL ACCIDENT AT PENYLAN MILLS.–A fatal accident of a dreadful character occurred on Wednesday morning, at Penylan Mills. A young man named John Edwards, aged seventeen, employed as under miller, in setting some of the machinery in motion in the upper story of the principal mill building, had to place a strap upon a pulley which revolved upon a horizontal shaft overhead. He ought to have used a step ladder specially provided for the purpose, and kept close at hand; instead of doing this, he imprudently stood upon a ledge, and while in this position he was caught by the strap and carried up to the rapidly-revolving shaft. The young man was instantly killed, and his body was shockingly mutilated. His clothes were torn off him, some wholly, and others in ribbons; his head was smashed, and one half of it was subsequently picked up at a distance of ten yards; his limbs were fractured, and there was scarcely a bone in his body that was not broken. Sometime afterwards the foreman, Thomas Jones, discovered the remains of the unfortunate young man, a ghastly spectacle, wrapped around the shaft.
December 29, 1869

1870 meant that the Advertiser had been published for 21 years:

At the beginning of a New Year we sometimes venture to write a few words about the past and future of the Advertizer; and on the present occasion we do so all the more readily because 1870 witnesses "the majority" of this journal. Twenty-one years ago the Advertizer made its appearance as a very small bantling [a young child] in the world of provincial journalism. It has grown in size: whether in wisdom and favour with men, our readers must judge.
January 5, 1870

There was some campaigning zeal by the Advertizer in this case:

AN INNOCENT MAN CONVICTED AT OSWESTRY.–On Thursday, two of Mr France's quarrymen, Richard Roberts and Henry Jones, were charged with trespassing on part of the Woodhill estate in search of rabbits on Christmas day. It is with Jones only did we have to deal. The sole evidence against the men was that of P.C.Salter; but, on the other hand, Henry Jones called three witnesses who bore independent testimony to the fact that he was far away from the place at the time the alleged offence was committed. Why the magistrates refused to believe those men we cannot say; but subsequent enquiries, carefully prosecuted by Mr France, have, we understand, established beyond doubt the truth of the alibi; and further than this, the person who was with Roberts, and who, we suppose, was mistaken for the unfortunate man now undergoing a sentence of three weeks' imprisonment, does not attempt to conceal the fact. A clearer case of injustice it is impossible to conceive, and Mr France, who has exerted

THE "STANDARD" PERFECT AS A REAPER.
IMPORTANT TRIAL OF MOWING MACHINES AT WRITHLINGTON.
FIRST PRIZE AWARDED TO PICKSLEY, SIMS, & CO.'S "STANDARD."

himself in a very praiseworthy manner in the interests of the prisoner, has carefully laid the facts before the magistrates.

Everyone agreed that it was Henry Jones's brother who was responsible, and even the brother admitted it; but Henry Jones was sent to prison. But it wasn't only the wrongful conviction that the Advertizer resented, but the laws on poaching, and who ruled on those laws:

What an odd and cruel thing it will seem to the Englishman of 1900, that only thirty years before, a person, summoned by a policeman-gamekeeper for being seen with a dog near a vermin hole, was sent by a bench of honourable country squires, who took a special interest in game, to an ignominious punishment, and, when his innocence was discovered, was unable to obtain his liberty! We fancy these ages, which seems so light to us, will look very dark to our descendants.
January 5, 1870

There is some comedy in this unfortunate incident:

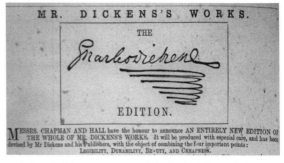

In June the Advertizer announced the death of Charles Dickens

TRAP ACCIDENT.–Mrs Moody, of St Martin's, accompanied by a friend, was seated in her market cart proceeding homewards, when opposite the Plough Inn a dog cart drawn by a spirited horse attempted to pass Mrs Moody's vehicle, which could not quickly enough be pulled on one side; the consequence was that the wheels of both became locked. The market cart was upset and so were the ladies, as well as a tin containing 42 lbs of treacle. The molasses, owing to the caving in of the bottom of the tin, descended with irresistible force upon the prostrate ladies, saturating their clothes. In this condition, they were taken into the Plough, and underwent a process of cleansing, which resulted in their being more presentable to public gaze. The cost of the treacle was paid by a gentleman who saw the accident.
January 26, 1870

A velocipede was an early type of bicycle without pedals; riders propelled themselves by pushing the ground with their feet:

Riding velocipedes, we presume, is an agreeable amusement, but it is certainly a dangerous one. Twice lately we have had to record velocipede accidents in the streets of Oswestry; and those who see these almost invisible vehicles rushing, in rather weirdlike style, through the town on a dark

night, must wonder greatly that casualties are not of constant occurrence. If the gentlemen who use these dangerous toys like to break their own legs by running against a lamppost in the darkness, we shall have little to say; but if they run over old women and children they must expect to pay rather dearly for their amusement.
April 27, 1870

Now that Oswestry had its Literary Institute, there was a move to have a town library too:

Our readers will be glad to learn that an effort is about to be made, with every hope of success, to establish a library that shall be worthy of the town, and really meet its requirements. A good collection of books has existed for some time at the Institute, but one far too small, so small, indeed, as to affect the prosperity of the institution; and the movement to which we refer aims at the extension of that library, with the addition of arrangement of permanently securing it to the town.
May 4, 1870

The strange thing here is being in court for throwing a stone into the canal, instead of for throwing what was attached to the stone:

Job Evans was summoned for throwing a stone into the Shropshire Union Canal, at Maesbury. The defendant and another person tied a large stone, weighing about 50 lbs, to a dog, and threw both dog and stone into the canal.–Defendant asserted that the stone was not in a part of the canal where it could interfere with the navigation, and that after the dog was drowned he took it out.–Case dismissed.
May 4, 1870

A different kind of stone throwing seems to have been prevalent in the town:

The dangerous practice of stone-throwing has grown to such a pitch in Oswestry that we hope the police will carefully direct their attention to it. Especially in the Horse Market is this mischievous habit indulged in, to the damage of property and the no small danger of neighbours and pedestrians. We are afraid a few summonses will have to be taken out before the evil is remedied.
May 25, 1870

One of the Advertizer's old campaigns was for the early closing of shops; at the Town Council meeting it was said:

A great drawback to early closing was the late closing of the market, and it was requested that the market should be closed at nine o'clock.–Mr Saunders: What! The market? Oh dear, no? (General cries of "No, no.") It would be so great an inconvenience to country people.–Mr J. Jones suggested that the market should be closed at half past nine, instead of half past ten, on Saturday nights.–The Town Clerk said it would not meet with

the approbation of the public, especially those people who, having perishable articles to sell, stopped until the very latest moment.
July 6, 1870

There was an unusual revelation, that there existed in Oswestry such a thing as 'baby farms':

On Thursday evening last an inquest was held on the body of Lizzy Jones, about a year and three months old, an illegitimate child, who died on the previous Tuesday. The attention of the police had been called to the case before the child died, and it was thought necessary to hold an enquiry on the body. The child had been put out to nurse at Elizabeth Plimley's, its mother living at Madeley; and since the child had been under the care of the woman Plimley, the mother had never seen it. In the mother's evidence, too, she appears to have doubts as to the exact period the child was born, and evidently cared little or nothing about it, and the jury thought fit to censure the mother as to her conduct in the matter.

This was the evidence:

Elizabeth Jones, the mother of the deceased, stated that she lived with her father, who is a builder living in the town of Madeley. The child remained

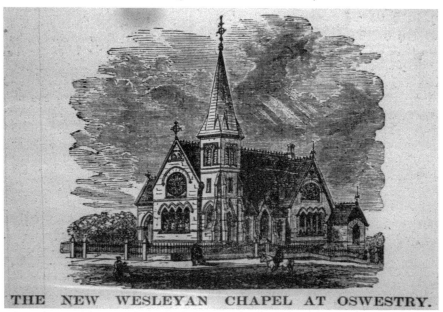

THE NEW WESLEYAN CHAPEL AT OSWESTRY.

This is the chapel that used to be on Beatrice Street (it was demolished in 1967), opposite the Plough Inn, where the BP filling station is now; it was also the site of Bickerton's Pool:
'THE NEW WESLEYAN CHAPEL.. The ceremonial of laying a chief corner-stone and four memorial stones in the edifice which is being erected for the Wesleyan Methodists at Oswestry took place on Thursday. A very large assembly congregated upon the interesting occasion.' June 15, 1870

with her sister about ten or eleven months, after which it was brought to Oswestry. The child was never in good health. Witness had not seen the child since it had been under the care of Mrs Plimley. Plimley had been paid two months for the child, and there was three months' pay owing at the time of the child's death.

The woman who had taken the child gave her account:

Elizabeth Plimley said–I am the wife of Frederick Plimley, Ostler, and lived in Black Gate. I had the child on the 17th of February last. The child appeared very ill at the time. I usually fed the child on corn flour and milk, and bread and milk. I never saw the mother.

Dr Beresford said–On opening the abdomen I found the stomach very largely dilated, and the walls very thin and transparent, but still the structure was healthy. It contained a small quantity of gruel-like fluid. I found no other disease. There was a great absence of fat in most of the intestines. I am of opinion that death resulted from chronic disease of the lung. I think the child was a delicate child in the first instance, and has been improperly nourished throughout – as a dilated condition of the stomach proves. I may remark, with reference to the room the child was in, two adults and five children slept in that room at night–there being hardly sufficient space for one. The hours which the child was in that poisoned atmosphere was sufficient to cause the diseased state of the lung, and recovery in such a place would be out of the question. I do not think I am stating it too strongly in saying so.

The jury, after consideration, returned the following verdict, "Died from natural causes accelerated by improper food and bad air."

The Advertizer made this comment on the case:

We have it on the authority of the Coroner, that there are "baby farms" in the town; and their inspection is an important public duty which the council, we are sure, will carefully discharge. The particular enquiry that led to the recommendation, although it revealed no criminal purpose or intentional unkindness on the part of the nurse, was sufficient to show the wretched life which many unfortunate children lead; and it is hardly too much to suppose that some of the Oswestry "baby farms" resemble similar establishments in large towns, where illegitimate children are taken in exchange for a good round sum of money, and then nursed to death. Infanticide in England, we fear, is a much more common and systematic thing that most people suppose.

July 13, 1870

As suspected, the waterworks proved insufficient:

As the drought continues, in the present unfortunate state of affairs, the Oswestry water supply becomes more and more inadequate to the requirements of the town. At the meeting of the Local Board on Monday attention was called to the fact, and it was ordered that the time during which

the water is turned on should be lessened by one hour.
August 3, 1870

This case seems to be persecution by the police, but we can only guess at what the 'unlawful purposes' were; it features a less than bright girl called Miss Scott:

A MOONLIGHT PICNIC.–David Edwards, labourer, John Morris, butcher, George Lamb, labourer, and Sarah Pritchard, characters well-known in police annals, were charged by Sergeant Thomas with being in a field for unlawful purposes. Sergeant Thomas said that early on Thursday morning he heard talking going on in the field, and thinking that the numbers were more than he could manage single-handed, he went back to town for a couple of officers. A rush was made into the field, and the party were found snugly ensconced in the bottom of a dry ditch, enjoying a bottle of rum. The party, which included a girl named Scott, were conveyed to the lock-up, but on the way Scott managed to break loose from the officers, bolted through the Horse Market, and was not to be found in time to rejoin the party in the Police Court. Edwards was committed for three weeks, Morris and Lamb to seven days, and Pritchard six weeks. In the course of the afternoon Miss Scott turned up on an errand of mercy, bringing refreshments to her quondam companions. She was politely invited into the lock-up by Sergeant Thomas, and to her surprise, the key was turned upon her. She was brought before the Mayor later in the day, and committed for six weeks; hard labour.
August 10, 1870

Another drunken case:

THE GENTLE SEX.–Caroline Smith, a peripatetic vendor of small wares, was brought up in the custody of Sergeant Thomas under the following circumstances. On the previous night she presented herself at the police station, and having disencumbered herself of her basket, she took off her shawl and bonnet, and pitched them at the sergeant's head. She was proceeding further to divest herself of her wearing apparel, when Thomas seized her, and with some difficulty got her into the lock-up. Whilst there she smashed every pane of glass in the window, and tearing a piece of wood from the bedstead, she knocked the window frame out. Having done this she undressed herself, and threw every vestige of clothing through the window, and made the night hideous with her noise. She appeared to be suffering from the effects of a heavy drinking bout, and when before the magistrates appeared very much ashamed of her conduct.
August 24, 1870

This is a strong comment on the laws against poaching:

In this free and happy country we can get drunk, annoy our neighbours, and beat our wives, all for less than half a sovereign; but if we trespass on our neighbours' fields, and touch the sacred feather of a partridge, a five

pound note hardly covers the cost of our diversion. At Wrexham police court, on Monday, two young men had to pay, one £3 19s, and the other £2 19s, for killing partridges. They might have almost killed a woman of the same sum.
September 28, 1870

This was the first patient for the new Cottage Hospital:

ACCIDENT AT THE NEW GAOL.–On Friday afternoon, an accident, fortunately unattended with any very serious results, occurred at the new gaol in course of erection in the Horse Market. A man named Joseph Broughall, a joiner living in Beatrice-street, was walking across the joists, when he slipped, and fell a distance of about 13ft. When picked up it was found that he was severely cut about his head and face, having fallen amongst the quantity of bricks, and that his nose was cut through by a slate. He had no business about the place, and the men employed upon the works, seeing that he was very drunk, had cautioned him against going up the ladder, and had once taken him down by force. He is the first patient who has been admitted to the new Cottage Hospital.
September 28, 1870

The continental war referred to is the Franco-Prussian War, which began in July:

AURORA BOREALIS.–A magnificent display of the Aurora Borealis was witnessed here on Monday night. The display attained its greatest brilliance about eight o'clock, when a deep crimson flush almost covered the heavens. Amongst the less educated portion of the community a connection was traced between this certainly dire looking portent and the continental war!
October 26, 1870

The frequently used tone of gentle irony is continued here:

SIR,–You may not have heard of the following accident. As one of the aldermen of the borough, accompanied by one of the town councillors, was walking through the Castle Fields a few nights ago, never having visited it before since the year 1850, they came upon the rope-walk bridge (still so called by courtesy, though nothing but a rotten plank remains of the former structure), and, not being aware of its unprotected condition, both gentlemen fell, on their heads I regret to say, on the walk below. Both sustained serious injuries, and –
I have written so far when I discovered that the accident was not yet enacted–of course it isn't, but the bridge remains unprotected, and you think it would if an alderman and a councillor had fallen over it? Or do you think the Castle Fields would remain as dirty and disorderly as they are?
ALIQUIS.
November 2, 1870

Here is another bad industrial accident:

A melancholy and fatal accident occurred at Mr Peate's, Weston Mills, on Friday morning, when a man named William Francis lost his life. It appears that the deceased, in company with a man named Lewis, was engaged in driving some iron wedges out of the water wheel. The wheel being insufficiently propped, was set in motion by the overflow from the water trough, and the poor fellow was carried down with the revolving wheel, and terribly crushed. His lifeless body was extricated in about half an hour after the occurrence of the accident. The deceased bore the character of a sober, steady, and industrious workman. He had been in the employ of Mr Peate for nearly twelve years, and has left a widow and five young children. *November 30, 1870*

The Advertizer finished the year by looking back on it, though in fact from a 21st century historical perspective it was not particularly significant for Britain:

1870.–The year which is closing will be remembered as one of the most memorable years of the present century. Events, at home and abroad, crowd upon one another so closely, that a bare enumeration of the more important is almost impossible within our present limits. *December 28, 1870*

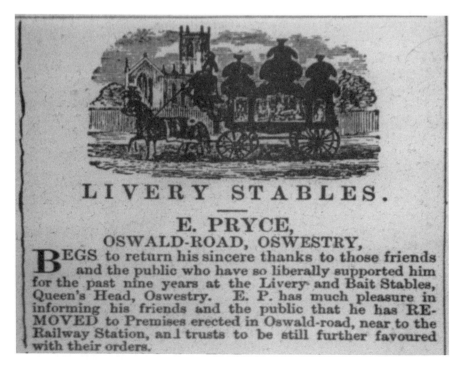

LIVERY STABLES.

E. PRYCE,
OSWALD-ROAD, OSWESTRY,
BEGS to return his sincere thanks to those friends and the public who have so liberally supported him for the past nine years at the Livery and Bait Stables, Queen's Head, Oswestry. E. P. has much pleasure in informing his friends and the public that he has RE-MOVED to Premises erected in Oswald-road, near to the Railway Station, and trusts to be still further favoured with their orders.

There is a strange unsolved mystery: today we read the ADVERTIZER, but in the period of this book they mostly read the ADVERTISER. When and why did the S change to Z? The when is easy. It occurred in July, 1869. This is the masthead of June 30:

And this is the masthead for July 7:

Inside the paper every reference to 'Advertiser'...

...is now to 'Advertizer':

But why this happened is harder to solve. I can find no explanation anywhere as to the reason for the change, nor is there a single letter or comment about it.

It seems at the time simply to have been neither noticed nor explained.

THOMAS SAVIN

THOMAS SAVIN was born in 1826, at Llwynymaen, between Oswestry and Trefonen. He started out as an apprentice draper in his father's shop, later becoming a partner in Messrs Morris & Savin of Cross Street. He married Elizabeth Hughes of Park Farm in 1852. They moved to Plasffynnon, along Middleton Road (now used by the Inland Revenue) and had the house enlarged and rebuilt.

He branched out from draping to being a hop merchant, and a grocer, and owning Coed-y-go Colliery, near Morda. But the new thing in Britain was railway building, and this seemed to attract him like nothing else, because for the rest of his life he described himself as a 'Railway Contractor'.

George Owen introduced Savin to David Davies of Llandinam (the man who built Barry Docks) in a room over the tobacconist shop opposite the old Post Office in Church Street, in the late 1850s. This significant meeting started their railway building partnership.

The list of railways Savin built, both with and without Davies, is impressive: the Llanidloes and Newtown, the Vale of Clwyd, the Oswestry and Newtown, the Mid Wales, the Machynlleth to Aberystwyth, the Kerry Branch, the Llanfyllin branch, the Hereford, Hay and Brecon, the Kington and Eardisley, the Brecon and Merthyr, and the Caernarfonshire Railways, among others.

In 1856 he entered Oswestry Town Council, and became a churchwarden. In 1863 he was appointed Oswestry Town Mayor, and around this time he began to build and buy hotels on the Welsh coast, including the sandstone neo-Gothic building in Aberystwyth that is now known as the 'Old-College', and the Cambrian Hotel at Borth. His idea was that the Cambrian Railways would become successful by transporting people of the West Midlands to the Welsh coast for their holidays.

But in 1866 everything crashed spectacularly. His estimate for the cost of the Machynlleth to Barmouth Railway was wildly low, because he hadn't realised that at Aberdovey the railway would need so many tunnels, there being no room between the town and the estuary for a line. His other problem was that instead of always taking money when he built railways he took shares. This meant he had a huge number of shares in a great number of companies all over Britain and the

Thomas Savin
(from The Story
of the Cambrian)

world. But contractors have to buy in goods and services, and the people that provide those goods and services demand money, not shares, and on February 5th so many people wanted money he was forced to declare himself bankrupt.

It was discovered he owed over £2 million, a huge sum for those days, the equivalent of several billion pounds now. His crash had an effect on the whole economy of the country, because he helped cause the collapse of Overend & Gurney's Bank (the last British bank to collapse before Northern Rock), which itself caused a recession in Britain.

When Savin's finances were sorted out, his shares were taken from him to pay his debts, though he was allowed to own four small companies: Porthywaen limeworks, Fenns Bank brickworks, Ynyslas brickworks at Borth, and Coedygoe Colliery.

He deserves to be remembered if for nothing else because without him Oswestry would stayed a small market town. He was the one who insisted that the railways works were built there, and not in Welshpool or near Newtown.

He died on the 23rd July, 1889, and was buried in Oswestry cemetery. He has recently been commemorated in Oswestry by the naming of a road, appropriately near the station: 'THOMAS SAVIN ROAD'.

George Owen (from The Story of the Cambrian)

GEORGE OWEN

GEORGE OWEN came from Tunbridge Wells. Making Oswestry his home as surveyor of the Oswestry District of roads, George Owen became a member of the Town Council in 1860, mayor in 1864 and 1865, and alderman in 1874. He then became resident engineer of the Cambrian Railways, an important position. For twenty years he was a member of the General Purposes Committee, served as borough and county magistrate, and was a member of the School Board from its inception, and chairman from 1891 till his death in 1901. He introduced Thomas Savin to David Davies, which began Savin's career as Railway King.

ON THE BORDER

The Story of Llanymynech & Pant

Neil Rhodes

FOREWORD BY LEMBIT ÖPIK MP